Y0-BRN-904

EMERSON'S RELEVANCE TODAY
A SYMPOSIUM

Edited by

ERIC W. CARLSON

AND

J. LASLEY DAMERON

TRANSCENDENTAL BOOKS—DRAWER 1080—HARTFORD 06101

TABLE OF CONTENTS

FOREWORD

I. EMERSON AND AMERICA TODAY

EMERSON'S MODERNISM—NEW INSIGHTS Eric W. Carlson 3

EMERSON AND THE THIRD AMERICA Reginald L. Cook 7

EMERSONIAN IDEAS IN THE YOUTH MOVEMENT OF THE 1960's Alfred S. Reid 12

EMERSON'S "YOUNG AMERICAN" AS DEMOCRATIC NOBLEMAN John Q. Anderson 16

II. MODERN ASPECTS OF EMERSON'S METHOD

EMERSON'S METHOD AS A PHILOSOPHER William B. Barton 20

FIRST PERSON SUPERLATIVE: THE SPEAKER IN EMERSON'S ESSAYS Lawrence Buell . . 28

III. EXISTENTIAL CRISIS AND RESOLUTION

THE CRISIS OF ALIENATION IN EMERSON'S EARLY THOUGHT Lewis P. Simpson . . . 35

EMERSON'S "INSTANT ETERNITY": AN EXISTENTIAL APPROACH Mary Edrich Redding . 43

IV. THE WORLD OF THE PSYCHE

EMERSON ON THE PSYCHIC POTENTIAL J. Russell Reaver 52

EMERSON AND THE WORLD OF DREAM Vivian C. Hopkins 56

PICTURES OF EMERSON—FAMILIAR AND UNFAMILIAR 70

COLOPHON 84

CORRECTIONS—ADDENDA

PAGE	LINE	
1	note	Professor Carlson wishes to acknowledge grant support from the University of Connecticut Research Foundation for duplication of materials.
4	46	studies,
9	6	method or point of view
12	32	...reference, but drawing also on limited but....
14	34	"...democratic process": "the substratum...."
19	44	"...recorded" (394-395).
28		[Omit the two opening sentences of Professor Buell's article and begin it with the following:] Emerson strongly anticipates the arguments for what is called "relevance"....
47	44	"All writing comes by the grace of God,"[36]
51	16	...1903-1904), I, 60.
51	29	p. 119, note 88.
53	40	so sorrow encroaches

FOREWORD

The present volume discusses Emerson as visibly or invisibly important today, wisely making no attempt to "modernize" him, which would be a perilous undertaking that would oversimplify and distort. He appears rather as an important part of the tradition within which much individual talent at its best currently expresses itself. As a significant part of America's "usable past," therefore, Emerson rightly deserves the revival we are beginning to observe on many fronts.

EMERSON'S MODERNISM

ERIC W. CARLSON

"Emerson is being studied afresh and found to have something to say that is relevant to our condition...it seems clear that at present Emerson is on the way to becoming the 'in' writer that Hawthorne has been for so long." So wrote Hyatt H. Waggoner in his 1970 introduction to the Rinehart Hawthorne: Selected Tales and Sketches. That the present collection of papers was conceived and assembled before his statement appeared underscores the truth of his first sentence. One is not so readily convinced, however, that Emerson is riding the high-tide of contemporary taste if that means that his work is now being read in depth by others than specialists. In editing this volume Professor Dameron and I operated from the view expressed by Reginald Cook in the opening essay: the modern generation is not quite sure that there are "truly radical insights" beneath Emerson's seemingly bland manner and lofty optimism. If "close readers of Emerson have other and contrary opinions," then, for the many, a "credibility gap" exists.

Professor Cook attributes this gap to the "superficial reading" that fails to see that if Emerson is a Platonist he is a Yankee Platonist, that if he is a cosmic idealist, he is also a skeptical humanist, a civilizer, and an intellectual awakener. Contrary to Stephen Whicher's view, Reginald Cook finds Emerson's belief in man just as firm at 68 as at 33. Moreover, he maintains, in our post-industrial age we shall not rise above the level of the technological man and the "organization man" without the moral courage and individualism of Emerson's inner-directed man. And yet Emerson's influence can also be measured by the "supreme holistic thrust" that made the journey of Apollo 11 an amazing example of "collective self-reliance."

Significantly, Alfred S. Reid's essay on the relevance of Emerson's ideas to those of the youth movement of the 1960's was only one of several such papers submitted or projected. Although most young activists may pass by Emerson as a non-action "liberal," a conservative gradualist, Reid finds "a solid core of Emersonianism" in the new-left youth ideology of the Sixties. Emerson understood the perpetual generation gap, and the alienation and frustration engendered by it. His analysis of the way the System tends to repress integrity and individualism "put him with Marx and Marcuse and the black revolutionaries" as one of "the intellectual godfathers" of the Youth Movement. Although reluctant to advocate political activism beyond the "tart tongue" of verbal protest, Emerson urged every man to be a "reformer" of "the whole of our social structure, the State, the school, religion, marriage, trade, science..." by "laying one stone aright every day," and by reliance on kindness, love, hope and faith, rather than on violence as a principle.

In his evaluation of "The Young American" John Q. Anderson illustrates how Emerson, as if trying to close the credibility gap of that day (1844), assumed the role of cultural critic and philosopher. He urged his young listeners to greater efforts of self-realization, not in the name of "Manifest Destiny" but in the spirit of practical idealism, "beneficent socialism," human destiny, and the true democratic "nobility" of self-reliant men. If these value-ideals have lost some of their power today, the barriers to self-reliance remain recognizably modern: materialism, poverty, the temptation to escape to Europe, a tendency to introversion, the failure of the government to be responsive to change, and the "conventional virtues" advocated by the public media and institutions. If forethought does not often characterize the young American today, others of Emerson's requisites do--a life "secretly beautiful," a concern for general justice and humanity, a "noble mind" inspired by a spirit of hope and liberality. Most relevant for the youth of the 1970's, according to Anderson, is the implication that "confrontation" must be made first with one's own non-negotiable integrity, and secondly with the principle that individuals acquire rights only as they accept responsibility, which means discipline.

Especially welcome to this collection is the essay on the modernism of Emerson's method by William B. Barton, a specialist in philosophy. Beginning with the observation that "the scrap-book view of Emerson's method of philosophizing has held the field too long," Professor Barton traces the development of Emerson's method, defines his conceptions of language, poetry, and science, and points up the relevance of that method to modern thought. "Emerson, in fact, was among the first modern philosophers to set forth the outlines of a thorough-going process philosophy of organism founded on evolutionary principles. In its ontological implications it is at least as imposing as Bergson or Whitehead." Emerson's strength lies in his generalizing the method of natural history and applying it to the whole of human experience. In saying 'I fully believe in both, in the poetry and in the dissection,' Emerson rejected the purely analytic or arbitrary as unable to catch life in process within a universe open, changing, and evolving; he rejected both analysis and introspection as mutually exclusive, self-sufficient modes of inquiry. Pushing beyond observation and generalization, he insisted in allowing the realized fact to reveal its own context or pattern of meaning, until Reality emerged as an organic process and whole. Barton concludes that Emerson completed his life-time task of "working out the Natural History of the Intellect."

Further evidence of Emerson's feeling for the quality of experience is to be had in Lawrence Buell's "First Person Superlative: The Speaker in Emerson's Essays." Comparing personae, Buell discovers the early Emerson to be vigorous and exciting, not diffuse, in his personal tone of realization; the later voice becomes less exemplary, giving way to the garrulous and the private in feeling or opinion. The truly personal speaker is a composite of the private, adding a sense of personal witness, circumstantial detail, etc., and of the universal or exemplary. In Nature, "Self-Reliance," and "Experience," the personal-universal passages epitomize the philosophy of the whole essay; the exemplary persona has a personality of its own, with imaginative reach and appeal.

The next pair of studies by Professors Simpson and Redding, set forth the ways in which Emerson came to grips with two problems central to the modern mind. According to Professor Simpson, Nature came as a sudden "dramatic manifesto asserting the radical freedom of the modern mind," the climax and resolution of a long crisis in Emerson's grappling with the relationship of knowledge as an institution and knowledge as consciousness, with knowledge as doubt and knowledge as wonder. In 1823-1824, Emerson began a deep questioning of rational Christianity and the whole rational approach to knowledge that depended on doubt. The crisis of Emerson's early thought was that of his age. In a Galilean metaphor--'Faith is a telescope'--Emerson affirmed that the potentials of faith and wonder could be inspired by radical new

perspectives, thus transforming his anxiety of alienation from the "world home" into a tremendous sense of psychic power. Hence, his own transparent-eyeball image functioned as "a radical metaphor of the power of the consciousness of consciousness," the restoration of wonder, clear vision, and control of the universe. Curiously, at this point in his essay, Simpson grants Emerson only a half-resolution of his alienation-crisis. By 1838, he holds, the new-found vision of sheer Becoming revealed its ironical cost--a chilling separation from the community of men. Proof of Emerson's failure to restore a sense of wonder to the modern psyche Simpson sees in the technological desecration of the moon, that great symbol of wonder. But if Man is seen as an organic part of a holistic Over-Soul of immanent goal-seeking life forces, surely there is more, not less, promise for the creative individual attuned to the potential of community experience and purpose, even in the face of the strongest contrary feelings, as Emerson made clear in the closing pages of "Montaigne; or The Skeptic" and "Fate."

In her essay, Mary Edrich Redding shows how Emerson resolved another personal and philosophical problem, that of "immortality" by redefining it experientially, if not existentially, in the full Kierkegaardian sense. In 1836, Carlyle's conception of "Eternity" as "a Now and Here" was essentially Emerson's intensive, depth-of-life, this-world view of the "soul" as realized experience culminating in the present. In discussing "Threnody" Redding distinguishes "the genuine existentially spontaneous experiencing of grief in the recollections of the details of Waldo's play, habits, and mannerisms" from the intellectualized grief of conventional expressions and the depersonalized resignation of 'Lost in God, in Godhead found.' The tendency to substitute a "structure" for the passion of confrontation dilutes Emerson's encounters with the Other, Professor Redding feels. But she grants that even if his spiritual encounters were in many ways "merely partial and negative," Emerson did have the very practical awareness of life as "prospective." She grants, too, that "It is not the passion itself, but the acceptance of the authenticity of passion that we learn from others," an authenticity expressed in Emerson's haunting challenge: "Whatever games are played with us, we must play no games with ourselves, but deal in our privacy with the last honesty and truth."

In order to draw fully on his "consciousness of consciousness," as Professor Simpson phrases it, Emerson not only had to go beyond the institutional and rational view of knowledge but, according to J. Russell Reaver, had to free himself from the blocks of the Tragic and the Comic. Regarding these as "the trap of an ego-centered attitude claiming that life offers only tragic defeat or absurd spectacle"--Professor Reaver describes the young Emerson as developing a "special faith in the creative unconscious...deep structures of mind, providing ideal sources of value," "a capacity superseding the tragic vision." This psychic potential operates among men as a creative Will in the elemental unconscious, out of the deep need for goodness and truth. Although man's sense of comedy may save him from insanity when confronted by an apparent cosmic joke, neither wit nor irony can compensate for the "wisdom and love" that transcend tragic or comic subjectivity. "After ridicule, lies wisdom. After tragedy, love remains," concludes Reaver.

Vivian Hopkins' pioneering study, "Emerson and the World of Dream," presents an unexpectedly rich documentation of Emerson's unconscious psyche. Erich Fromm's comment on the essay "Demonology" can be applied also to these dream-experiences: "Emerson's statement is significant because he recognizes more clearly than anyone had recognized before him the connection between character and the dream."

In an analysis by Hopkins of seventeen dreams between 1832 and 1867, only one was pleasant, five philosophical, the remainder grim, grotesque, and the like. Where "turbulent" visions occur, they range from a fear of immoderate laughter, to anxiety over his marriage, to dread of the ultimate. In this context of noting that hideous dreams reflect the dreamer's own "evil passions" Emerson wrote: "The good that he sees compared to the evil that he sees is as his own good to his own evil," a context overlooked by Melville in denouncing this statement. Several dreams illustrate the collective unconscious, whether as a feeling of sublime power, or of flight (creativity, transcendence), or of the mysterious unknown. Although Emerson held that such divination "resounds everywhere," he recognized that "Demonology is the shadow of theology." Though he distrusted "the gypsy principle" he studied his dreams in an effort to understand himself and the creative imagination. He was fascinated by them--the double consciousness symbolized in some, the synthesizing and censuring power in others, and the prophetic or philosophical character in still others.

Through these nine essays, Emerson's significance today can be appreciated in several areas of value--political, social, cultural, psychological, as well as literary and philosophical. If they represent--

as I think they do--a fair cross-section of new insights into Emerson's mind and contribution, then Professor Waggoner seems entirely justified in writing that "Emerson is being studied afresh and found to have something to say that is relevant to our condition...." In a symposium of this kind, where none of the contributors knows what the others have submitted, it is especially a matter of surprise and significance that several papers should deal with the psychic power and potential in Emerson's view of man, and several others with the cultural and the philosophical relevancies of his ideas. All in all, this symposium offers another striking illustration of the significance and value to be found in Emerson's work.

University of Connecticut

EMERSON AND THE THIRD AMERICA

REGINALD L. COOK

"To be an American is of itself almost a moral condition, an education, and a career." George Santayana, Character and Opinion in the United States.

Already there is something a little legendary about Emerson. He has long been one of us but with a difference. If the modern generation has "a thing" about him, it contrasts sharply with a more favorable view of Emerson's fellow Concordian Thoreau, who is felt to have "soul." No one doubts the sincerity of Emerson's affiliation with the Transcendentalists. But when Mrs. B., as noted by Emerson, described Transcendentalism with a wave of the hand, as "a little beyond," she put a handy stick with a clout in the arsenal of the anti-Transcendentalists. No phrase more aptly evokes the vagaries of a movement tending toward nebulosity than "a little beyond." Emerson's believing temperament and Transcendentalism appear to be a matched team. Yet at times critics considered the orbitry of his eloquence too exalted, facile and, at last, suspect. George W. Cooke, in an Emerson study published in 1887, quotes a writer in the Princeton Review who thought the essays "could be produced through a lifetime as rapidly as a human pen could be made to move."

A modern generation less enthusiastic about Transcendentalism than an earlier one is not quite sure what the essays mean in changing times. Are there truly radical insights beneath the bland manner and lofty optimism? In Melville, Hawthorne, and Thoreau the modern generation finds more compatible intellectual interpreters. There is apparently an Emersonian credibility gap. The essays in which the modern generation finds the Journals a little "let out," read as though Emerson began them when a relatively young man and finished them relatively unchanged. Close readers of Emerson have other and contrary opinions on his growth and development.

A segment of the older generation with a longer memory reads Emerson somewhat in the spirit of Holmes, Lowell, and William James, all of whom heard inspirational trumpet blasts in the Concordian. Their memories extend not to the best days in the early Republic, but to the only days--the epoch of the American Renaissance, the golden day, the flowering of New England. They respond to one of our tribal voices with a trumpet attachment, whose cautionary essays and poems resonate with exhortation. "So nigh is grandeur to our dust.... The youth replies, I can."

Earlier in this century two views of Emerson were incisively presented by Henry Adams and George Santayana. In the Education (1907), Adams professes to be troubled by Emerson's inability to recognize the chasm of the times. If Webster had not seemed to protest much, Emerson protested even less. For this failure Adams finds Emerson "naif." Typically, this is the sophisticated Adams' way of faulting the Concordian's sublime unconsciousness, noting a defect in intellectual percipiency, not, certainly, of moral character. Emerson issued no caveats, raised no tribal voice, blew no warning trumpet blasts, to keep us from rapid descent into the inferno of twentieth-century multiplicity and the symbolic waste land.

Another incisive view of Emerson is in George Santayana's Interpretations of Poetry and Religion (1900). "A Puritan mystic with a poetic fancy and a gift for observation and epigram" sums up his appraisal of the Concordian. Different from but not exclusive of the implications in Adams' view, Santayana's commentary is essentially reductive. Emerson does have deep Puritan roots, by right of birth and by both moral and intellectual attachment. "What a debt is ours to that old religion," he admits warmly in "The Method of Nature." But Santayana's phrase 'poetic fancy' is reductive. If you are a non-Calvinistic Puritan and your religion is 'poetic fancy,' you might just as well stick with the Unitarians. More than this, of course, is implied in Santayana's statement. He is really contending that Emerson's originality is not in thought but in style. Addicted to "the diction of ages," the scion of the Puritans is using it to give old and imperishable thoughts a particular beatific quality.

If the qualified views of Adams and Santayana are kept in mind, we might come closer to clarifying

Emerson's relevance today by adding an historical perspective. In Character and Opinion in the United States, Santayana makes a provocative reference to two Americas. The first of these is composed of "all the prodigals, truants, and adventurous spirits that the colonial families produced." The second reenforces the "truly native" by "the miscellany of Europe arriving later, not in the hope of founding a godly commonwealth, but only of prospering in an untrammalled one."

Yet isn't there a third America? In the historical metamorphosis it rests on a foundation of "austere principles" (of the first America), and it is populated by a miscellaneous group (of the second America) who discovered in a new land a new-found freedom from old-world restraints. Conditioned by a capitalistic economic system harnessed to an electronic technology, the twentieth-century citizen of the third America survives so far in a nuclear space age. The central fact in the perspective of the three Americas--the genteel, the miscellaneous (Jewish, Irish, German, Italian, "or whatever they may be"), and the electronic-oriented--poses the perennial identity problem. What does it mean to be an American? Henry James was not thinking wholly of an earlier time when he reminded us how complex the fate of being one was. His concern was with separation from the responsibilities of our old European home and the "superstitious valuation" attached to it. In 1920 Santayana up-dated "the complex fate." "To be an American," he wrote, "is of itself almost a moral condition, an education, and a career." In the mid-nineteenth century Emerson might have made this judgment without qualification. To be an American to Emerson is a moral condition, a religious education, and a dedicated career.

No one expects Emerson to have anticipated the enigmatic key problems of our time. And least of all no one would turn to him for calculated solutions to them. If anyone should make this demand of him, he is certainly unreasonable. Like others Emerson could make appropriate guesses. Shrewdly he could join two practical notions and foresee the obsolescence of another. "When," he recorded in 1843, "the rudder is invented for the balloon, railroads will be superseded." Now we have the crowded air of the jet age and faltering railroads. Or, in 1851, he might be said to have anticipated the contest between the RAF and the Luftwaffe in the Battle of Britain in World War II. "The attention of mankind is now fixed on ruddering the balloon, and probably the next war--the war of principle--is to be fought in the air."

Emerson, a modest man, was no soothsayer. The source of his oracular manner was divination, not prophecy. Most prophets are poseurs or attitudinizers. "When the spirit of prophecy comes upon you," Mark Twain satirized in A Connecticut Yankee, "you merely cake your intellect and lay it off in a cool place for a rest, and unship your jaw and leave it alone; it will work itself: the rest is prophecy." Obviously Emerson has little of Mark Twain's "spirit of prophecy." Early and late he was no advocate of economic reform, or of a Utopian social world as envisaged by the numerous associations of his time, including Brook Farm and Fruitlands. Nor was he a notional addict of Graham bread or hydropathy, phrenology or mesmerism.

The master question is: How can Emerson best help us confront the searching problems of the third America in which industrialized democracy is hemmed in by problems? In an epoch of ICBM's, suburban ghettos, conservation and pollution, we are confronted with the violence of nationalistic struggles, a dangerously increasing incidence of psychotic behavior, enforced loneliness from social maladjustment, the impatient struggle of ethnic groups for status recognition, a general permissiveness of relaxed morality, and the restraining and redirecting of man's aberrant instincts. Paradoxically, in the greatly expanded and spatially contracted world community in which we find ourselves, our financial aid is diligently sought and our capitalistic system is regarded with alarming suspicion.

The third America is incredibly energetic, "revved up," quantitative in its measurements, conspicuous in consumption, puzzling in its paradoxes, magnificently exciting in its moon-shots. Yet Santayana has a point in his conception of American identity as a "moral condition," and Emerson's relevance must be seen in these terms. If our morality has changed from life by principle so endemic to the "first America," or from the tactic of expediency typical of the second, is it not imperative to consider more than ever before in what that "moral condition," or the lack of it, consists? Emerson might conceivably represent the exhorter of moral goodness in the "Neon Wilderness." He might be one who, seer-like, helps us to re-identify that condition. Or, he might have a truly therapeutic effect in his cautionary essays, helping to heal the spirit--a magus healer, indeed.

The Emerson to whom we look for help may be legendary but exactly how "dated" is he? (1) Less a romantic quester than a reminder of our lost ideal, he is a steady and serene New England Yankee idealist, identified by clear and sufficient convictions. The vocabulary of his eupeptic temperament can be summed up in the assertion of moral energy--in conscience, self-reliance, virtue. Because of a native Yankee prudence and shrewdness, he is less a Transcendentalist, which amounts to a "digestion of vacancy" in Santayana's phrase, and more a Transcendentalist in the sense of having a method of point of view from which the world could be approached rather than a system of the universe. "I have no System," he reminded us emphatically. As a Yankee Platonist, his real world is not spatial and temporal only but inner and eternal. When, in "Experience," he says the Fall of Man is our discovery that we exist, that we inhabit the realm of time, he implies a disjunction between Plato's world of ideas, which is real, and our human condition which, because of the separation, is one of illusion and unreality. Yankee like, he counterbalances the abstract world of idea and the empirical world of thing. Like needles of light, his insights stitch together these two worlds in what he called bi-polarity.

In Psyche and Symbol, when discussing "the Phenomenology of the Spirit in Fairy Tales," Carl Jung states: "There is a deep doctrine in the legend of the Fall; it is the expression of a dim presentiment that the emancipation of ego consciousness was a Luciferian deed." Before the Fall, that is, in the unconscious or pre-conscious--before the ego became self-willed--there was no inner conflict between instinctiveness and human ego assertion, or arrogance. Emerson gives the Fall a Christian reading. "It is very unhappy," he says, "but too late to be helped, the discovery that we have made that we exist. That discovery is called the Fall of Man." Emerson's "existence" is the equivalent of a discovery that we have a lower self which warps the divinity. In his symbolic Fall, unlike Jung's, we do not "fall" from a primitive pre-conscious state into a rational consciousness but from a supreme unitary state of innocence into the divided state of experience where the conflict between animal and God is joined. The magic word for Jung's dualism of consciousness and unconsciousness is synthesis, or entelechy, which is an immanent agency directing our vital processes. I find relevant in this distinction a continuing awareness that from Emerson's position we do not progress irrevocably from one stage (preconscious) to another (conscious). We are daily confronted by the inevitable choice between the law for man and the law for thing. Our existence for better or for worse places the matter of choice in our hands. This is our moral condition.

(2) A superficial reading of Emerson discloses concern with cosmic rather than terresterial weather. A more searching look reveals a deep veining of granitic common-sense. In distrust of the scientific method, he runs the colors of an avowed skepticism up the jackstaff. "I distrust," he declared in 1844, "the facts and the inferences." But I cannot believe he as a humanist would fail to grow into the vision and responsibilities of our time. It is not the Emerson whose life falls casually between certain calendrical dates in the nineteenth century of whom we must think, but the humanist with insights and biases (by which he meant tendencies of temperament). "What at first scares the Spiritualist [we would say 'Fundamentalist' today] in the experiments of Natural Science...is impregnated with thought and heaven, and is really of God, and not of the Devil, as he had too hastily believed." This Emerson wrote in his Journals on February 10, 1871, when he was nearly sixty-eight.

Even more daringly he introduced his modest remonstrance to the Spiritualist by stating a position as applicable today as the moonshot or the heart transplant: "I do not know that I should feel threatened or insulted if a chemist should take his protoplasm or mix his hydrogen, oxygen, or carbon, and make an animalcule incontestably swimming and jumping before my eye. I should only feel that it indicated that the day had arrived when the human race might be trusted with a new degree of power, and its immense responsibility; for these steps are not solitary or local, but only a kind of an advanced frontier supported by an advancing race behind it." His trust in man was just as firm at sixty-eight as it was at thirty-three. Self-trust is that iron string which he vibrated truly. Perhaps we might say without demurrer that Emerson has raised the stakes, betting on man's ability to create life in the test tube, his exemplar being Dr. Gregory Pincus. Yet we notice his trust is based on "the advancing race" (my italics)--on the implication of qualitative, not quantitative measurement. It is a God-impregnated race, one in which the moral condition is salutary and energetic. Wholeheartedly the humanist he says: "Let man serve law for man; / Live for friendship, live for love."

(3) As a civilizer, Emerson's "hero" is neither a crusading knight nor a captain of industry. He is a self-contained man whose virtue implements the good, the true, the beautiful. To this voluntaristic

Concordian the impulses of the morally civilized originate in obedience to the Over-Soul. If this great and deep principle intensifies Emerson's eloquence and inaccessibility, if it makes him appear a little lacking in human warmth and fellowship, it has its compensatory direction, thrust, serenity. A sense of the ennobling relationship to the Over-Soul is the poetry of his existence. A non-conformist of the purest sort, he does not take God out of Heaven; he only finds Him within man. Upon returning from Europe in 1833, he informed his former congregation: "Man begins to hear a voice...that fills the heavens and the earth, saying that God is within him, that there is the Celestial host." Emerson's gentle manner delivers us from self-righteous dogmatism, from the Spanish Inquisitors, the Calvins, the Robespierres. Neither logician nor dialectitian--and notably no disputant-- he has in him more of Bernard of Clairveaux and William of Champeaux than of Abelard. He is more concerned with the love of God than the logic; he is more the man of the cloister than of the schools. He does not overstate his case when he admits: "I have no infirmity of faith."

Because he had deep clerical roots and inherited the genteel tradition, he communicates the traits of the believing temperament. Since he is a born believer, what appeals to him is moral beauty--the awareness of the good and true--moral energy. Everything he sees confirms ultimately the vision of the Over-Soul. To his disciple Confucius said: "'Ah, Sze, do you suppose that I merely learned a great deal and tried to remember it all?' The disciple said: 'Yes, isn't that what you do?' And Confucius replied: 'No, I have a system or a central thread that runs through it all.'" Similarly, Emerson's central thread was the Over-Soul, variously identified as Moral Sentiment or Identity, Universal Law, or the All. "And when, by and by, for an instant, the air clears and the cloud lifts a little, there are the gods still sitting around him on their thrones,--they alone with him alone."

I find both a relevance and an irrelevance in Emerson's moral posture as a civilizer. His religious view of history fails, it seems to me, to admit of the possibility of ultimate disaster by man-made means. He was not, of course, a political prophet. How, or why, should he anticipate Hiroshima? And he shows less wit than I should have expected in the long view of the World Soul; less wit, I think, than I find in the escape clause in Robert Frost's "It Bids Pretty Fair:"

> "The play seems out for an almost infinite run.
> Don't mind a little thing like the actors fighting.
> The only thing I worry about is the sun.
> We'll be all right if nothing goes wrong with the lighting."

Emerson's intransigence was religious; his vision, idealistic. Beneficent tendency seems no very satisfactory answer to such alternatives to thermonuclear war as unilateral disarmament or diplomatic strategy. What is disturbing is not so much the emphasis he places on the prevalence of virtue as his overlooking our sins. Not the assertion of virtue but the lack of self-criticism renders man vulnerable. The results are unfortunate when we exercise the soul at the expense of relaxing the intellect. Emerson's central insight--I am God ("as a plant in the earth so I grow in God. I am only a form of him. He is the soul of me. I can even with a mountainous aspiring say, I am God...")--was not fragile but deep and abiding. It was aimed at the heart of man because it is there that change must come. A vigorous segment of American literature--Melville and Hawthorne, Thoreau and Whitman, Mark Twain and Henry James, Sidney Lanier and Emily Dickinson--have urged this gospel. If they are irrelevant--fail to speak to us or cease to be heard--then Emerson is also irrelevant.

(4) As an intellectual awakener, Emerson's influence is both positive and negative. Today we find the transcendental way of receiving experience by total immersion in supraconsciousness neither easy nor acceptable. The modern citizen does not orbit in the reaches of the transcendental radiation belt, wherein it is always high noon and the sun very bright. Accustomed to face tragic events and stubborn issues for which there are few ready answers our generation grows impatient with bland optimism. How, for example, is the arms race to be slowed down, genocide prevented, tribalism eliminated, over-population controlled, the identity crisis of socialism to be resolved? And, at home, how are we to handle racism, poverty, welfare, transportation, and the war against crime?

Nevertheless, even when Emerson appears an innocent, whose chronic assurance appears to originate in temperament rather than in experience, he forces us to re-examine our position. No matter how

bland and sanguine he seems as an unterrorized perceiver of "the terror of life," he keeps the smug as well as the alert reader a little off balance. One wonders: "Does he try to reconcile or does he, as Henry Adams thought, blithely ignore facts contrary to theory? Does a vigorous exaltation of the upper half of life--the realm of Reason--only bring the needs of the lower half more acutely into view?" If he refuses to be engagé with some of the quickening social movements of his own time--like the Anti-Slavery Abolitionists--is he thereby immobolized by vis inertiae? If he prefers not to join organizations like Brook Farm is he then a Bartleby? If he is not a bristling antagonist, like the pawky Thoreau, is he sufficiently formidable as a detached protagonist? Does he show a bold tough-mindedness? Or is his affirmative nerve only negatively exercised?

On the positive side Emerson is an intellectual awakener whose gentle reticence belies association with "the soldiery of dissent." If he does not sport a red cockade like Wordsworth or Blake, at least he calls sharply in question the counting-house orthodoxy of State Street by rejecting "the pale negations" of Unitarianism, which, he thought, confounded important matters; substance was spirit, not matter. Spirit "does not build up nature around us but puts it forth through us." Nor, for him, was man a self-determining agent. Belief in such a doctrine might readily lead to arrogant ego-centrality. "The weakness of the will begins," he assumed, "when the individual would be something of himself." The self-relying individual draws moral strength from the Over-Soul, not from willful assertiveness. In this context, Emerson unshackled man from convention and timidity, invigorating and arousing him to non-conformistic action in rejection of inadequate creeds, dead forms, and superstitious rituals.

The relevance of Emerson has been suggested as a Yankee idealist, humanist, civilizer, and intellectual awakener. But in view of our remarkable success with the Apollo moonshot, what is his relevance today? When the astronomer I. M. Levitt, director of the Fels Planetarium of Philadelphia's Franklin Institute, heralds colonization of the moon, and former NASA Administrator Thomas Paine foresees future vacations on the moon for the affluent at about $5,000 the round trip, isn't it time to ask the important question? What difference does it really make whether we encourage space flight and establish lunar bases as the news media suggest, to project "an intergalactic Noah's ark that would carry a complete civilization to nearby stars," if we only infect the celestial realm with misdirected energies? How long will it take, say, to pollute Mars or Venus? We might stop to consider what the scientists already know, that technological man has drawbacks. At a recent London conference on pollution, a botanist from Washington University in St. Louis said: "A new generation is being raised--with DDT in their fat, carbon monoxide in their systems and lead in their bones. That is technological man." Is he, in short, the third American?

What is applicable in Emerson in the third America is not only the assertion of moral individualism but the application of the concept of individualism to a collective effort as well. Where the aims of a team or group are nobly conceived and scrupulously as well as intelligently followed, one finds a new and enlarged accommodation to Emerson's moral individualism. "What thou wouldst highly, that wouldst thou holily," applies here. The flight of Charles Lindberg on May 20-21, 1927, from Mineola to Paris is an exhilarating example of Emersonian self-reliance. But so too is the account of Apollo 11 on its 251,000-mile eight-day flight from Cape Kennedy to the amazing walk on the moon and splash-down in the Pacific--a remarkable example of collective self-reliance.

The twentieth-century technological age has successfully tested the truth that scientific brains can raise man to the moon and perspectives beyond. The remarkable coordination of the NASA laboratory at Houston, Texas, is the sum of multiple individual effort coordinated in a supreme holistic thrust with moral implications. In Santayana's words, what is applicable in Emerson today--his ultimate relevance--may be simply and sufficiently "new approaches to old beliefs or new expedients in old dilemmas." The new approach is the fresh way of expressing our spiritual resources. If this can be called religion, then it is one not afraid of science. It does not dishonor God and commit suicide.

Middlebury College

EMERSONIAN IDEAS IN THE YOUTH MOVEMENT OF THE 1960'S

ALFRED S. REID

Emerson is one of the uncelebrated god-fathers of today's protest movement. If we look only at his reluctance to engage in practical politics, we see no connection. If we look only at rowdy riots on streets and campuses, we see no connection. What could be further from Emersonian self-reliance and high-minded ethics than to burn records, lock deans in closets, or throw stones at policemen? Emerson believed that physical force would not transform power into practice, that man had to wait for the Over-God to marry right to might. He deplored mob action. Yet affinities exist between Emerson's social thought and that of the youth movement. I came forcibly to this realization, although like others I had thought of it before, at a midnight dormitory bull session last spring when several students consistently and angrily accused the older generation of hypocrisy in their various official roles as parents, teachers, administrators, politicians, and community leaders. The more I listened to charges of what amounted to a conspiracy of age and authority against youth, minorities, and general justice, the more I was reminded of Emerson's similar accusations. "Society everywhere is in conspiracy against the manhood of every one of its members. Society is a joint-stock company, in which the members agree, for the better securing of his bread to each shareholder, to surrender the liberty and culture of the eater. The virtue in most request is conformity."[1]

Neither the male students at the bull session, nor students in classes, nor those in radical youth groups, black or white, look directly to Emerson for their ideas. If asked, they regard him as a timid graybeard, an outmoded individualist, a hypocritical spokesman of the capitalistic establishment of last century. Some of the more seasoned youth theoreticians make a few ceremonious nods in Emerson's direction. Carl Oglesby says, "There is something very Emersonian about SDS." Jack Newfield agrees: "Historically, the New Radicals' forebearers are the Whitman-Emerson-Thoreau transcendentalists, and the...Wobblies." But mainly, Newfield says, the movement grew "up outside of all existing radical traditions."[2] It thus looks to more contemporary models--to Albert Camus' existentialism, to the neo-Marxist ideologies of Mao Tse-Tung and Che Guevara, and to black revolutionaries like Malcolm X. Especially influential is Herbert Marcuse's analysis of the "advanced industrial state." Since Newfield's study of the movement in 1967, it seems to have abandoned even the vestiges of the "humanist liberal tradition" of Emerson and Thoreau, of Mahatma Gandhi and Martin Luther King, and of other moderates who nourished its earlier phase. Sometime in the mid-60's, moral outrage and passive resistance turned militant.

Despite these new and more radical influences, today's new-left ideology of youth carries with it, as Newfield and Oglesby said, a solid core of Emersonianism. These ideas are central to the American experience. Young people have absorbed them, as their elders did, at home, church, and school. The chasm between the Emersonian tradition and the youth movement is more deceptive than real. Using Herbert Marcuse's One-Dimensional Man (1964) as something of a basic frame of written reference, but first-hand experience with several student activists in the past two years, I should like to point out three crucial ideas in today's movement that reflect a kinship, undefined but still viable, with some of Emerson's social ideas: the generation gap, the conspiracy theory of a repressive system, and the absolute necessity of reform. Obviously this approach is selective and exploratory. It is intended only as another item of evidence to support the contention that Emerson has continuing significance and relevance in American culture.

One of the Emersonian ideas in the movement is a sense of something wrong in the land and of the causal relationship of this wrongness to the tired corruptibility of old age. There is something rotten in the state of Denmark, something awry in the social system, and the older generation is to blame. There is corruption in high places, vicious crimes against humanity. Injustice prevails as part of the fabric of society; the established authorities condone it and practice it. The war in Vietnam is inhumane and irrational; the enemy is a fiction. Washington's preoccupation with kill-ratios has frayed the moral fibers of the nation. Racial discrimination is as vicious as ever. Defense spending takes money from the ghettoes. The draft is unfair to both poor and blacks and perpetuates discrimination and the war. Universities have sold their birthrights for defense contracts. There is a credibility gap as well as a generation gap.

The government and the news media withhold the truth. America is on the verge of becoming a police state. The youth cry, "Nobody is doing anything about it--all these wrongs." The establishment is outmoded and is not to be trusted. "Don't trust anyone over thirty," cry the youth. "Old men have been in power so long and have such vested interests that they are beyond help. They don't even see what's wrong. If they do, they lie and deceive to get rich. If the country ever does anything about these wrongs, young men will have to take over and restructure society from top to bottom."

Emerson sensed a similar generation gap. Society had become such a "colossus" of conservatism that the system needed total revision.[3] "In America, out-of-doors all seems a market; in-doors an air-tight stove of conventionalism."[4] New forms and structures were necessary, but the older generation had exhausted itself and was not equal to the task of reform. "Experience can never meet the new case.... Experience is only good in its beaten track." It remained for the youth, unencumbered by experience, prejudices, and property, to cope with life's problems and with "incessant change," which is the "condition of life and mind." "I have heard," said Emerson, "that after thirty a man wakes up sad every morning." Youth has energy and hope; age is timid and worn by ennui. It is already victim of a system that has sapped its initiative and coarsened its principles and driven it like a stake into the granite of inertia and prudent decorum. "Out of this measuring and decorum and prudence what refreshment can ever issue?"[5] The two main factions in society are separated in large measure by age. "The youth, of course, is an innovator by the fact of his birth;" the "upholder of the establishment" is older and more experienced but has grown conservative and defends and rationalizes the way things are. Youth senses that he has his own "thing" to do: "My genius leads me to build a different manner of life from any of yours." He regards age and the establishment as an obstacle in the path of self-fulfillment primarily because age is subservient to the profit motive and to private property: "To the end of your power you will serve this lie which cheats you."[6] Thus "The Present and the Past are always rivals.... Old and New set their seal to everything in Nature."[7] If there is change, it will have to come from youth: "All the children of men attack the colossus in their youth."[8] "I call upon you, young men, to obey your heart, and be the nobility of this land."[9]

A second idea held in common is, of course, the conspiracy theory of a repressive society. New-left youth, and many not affiliated with radical groups, see the government as an enemy of civil rights and justice, ignoring alike the challenge of youth and minorities. Authority is not only monolithic and entrenched, but corrupt and repressive. A colossal "military-industrial complex" is all-powerful. A slimy advertising culture pollutes the source of life. Hypocrisy and greed maintain the establishment against freedom, youth, hope, love, and peace. A college which espouses democratic ideals but which does not eliminate ghettoes or poverty or racial discrimination is guilty of these crimes against humanity. Academic requirements, social rules, and speaker policies are evidence of repressive measures to preserve the status quo and cancel the ideals of an education to free the spirit. Student language is not always sophisticated: "They keep us under thumb; they won't give minorities their rights. It's a closed society. They give us busy work or draft us to keep us from getting at the really important issues and values. They think the only goal in life is to succeed in the marketplace. Well, we refuse. We want a more meaningful life than the system gives us, one that relates to us as persons."

In a more sophisticated analysis, Herbert Marcuse calls the system the "advanced industrial society." Democracy and technology have given us such material progress that we have enslaved ourselves to them to keep progressing. A foreign "Enemy," which is built into the system, also keeps up the high standard of living. These forces, aided by public media, serve to "contain" social change by repressing critics and by keeping people preoccupied with what exploits them. The "New conformism" has whittled down the inner dimension so that a citizen is prevented from living the good life by palliatives, by the material goods that he thinks are the good life. He has become one-dimensional; he lives only to serve the system. All else is repressed.[10]

Emerson's analysis of society in "The Present Age" is very similar to that of Marcuse's. People are bound to a progressive political and economic system that holds out the promise of gratification. Since the "majority of men live chiefly to their senses...the conspicuous effect of freedom must be the multiplication and improvement of all fruits and instruments that serve the senses, the swarm of inventions in the useful, ornamental, and luxurious arts...." But these advances lead to domination over men. Emerson's term for repression and containment is decorum. Citizens, he says, are under the "domination of fashion" and of "the leading class in the capital" and thus substitute "decorum for the sinews of virtue and

intellect.... Decorum is a sign of the inaction of the higher faculties.... Decorum is a perfect passport. Decorum shall keep you from dirk and pistol, from mob and Committee of Safety, from profanity and obscenity, from sheriff and watchman." But the price is high: loss of integrity and individualism. "Decorum is a cloak that covers all." It obscures "the worthier objects of living." For "all this good [of gratification of senses through trade and technology] does not exist without some alloy." It "overpowers" the higher nature and makes a man "unscrupulous in the means." Trade is corrupting. "The noble sentiments of loyalty and patriotism are outraged by seeing power and law at auction and the conscience of the citizen seared." It especially conceals hypocrisy in high places: "You shall hear in debates where a gentleman shall speak and make as if he was in earnest with pathetic tones and gesture...and all about nothing." It also dulls the faculties of protest. "The speculative ability of the time feels the bribe of wealth and men of genius are tempted to betray their high priesthood and quit the duty of watching and imparting their own word for the more gainful office of gratifying the popular tastes."[11] Thus the system "contains" social change because it enslaves people to participate in activities which forever demand more of the same. To the extent to which the system achieves its material goals, to that extent are citizens slaves.

A third idea shared by Emerson and the movement is the necessity and duty of reform. The students say, "We want control over the course of our private lives; we want autonomy so we can cultivate our own interests, do our own thing, improve the quality of our lives and that of others around us. Piecemeal reform is inadequate. We must change society. Nevertheless, we have to start somewhere. So we'll start by eliminating obvious injustices close at home. Ordinary channels of communication are closed or lead nowhere. All the establishment does is listen; it never acts. Only by confrontation can we get anywhere. Whatever it takes--organizations, marches, protests, sit-ins, submitting of petitions, manning the barricades--we'll do it."

Marcuse recognizes four steps to liberate ourselves from ourselves and from our capitalist masters. First, we must be conscious of the system's repressiveness and of the absolute need of breaking out of the trap. "All liberation depends on the consciousness of servitude. Second, we must replace false needs provided by the system with new needs, true ones, provided both from within and from without. Unfortunately, we have become so mutilated in spirit that we no longer have the necessary inner values. Therefore, third, we shall have to go beyond psychology and ethics into politics. The main solution to qualitative change is "central planning," for the "goal of authentic self-determination by the individual depends on effective social control over the production and distribution of the necessities." "The job is a technical one:" "the planned utilization of resources for the satisfaction of vital needs with a minimum of toil, the transformation of leisure into free time, the pacification of the struggle for existence." Fourth, the conflict between domination and self-determination may have to be blatant: "material force is necessary," especially the force of organized confrontations by those "outside the democratic process:" the substratum of the outcasts and outsiders, the exploited and persecuted of other races and other colors, the unemployed and unemployable...."[12]

Emerson's commitment to reform is just as total, but is not predicated on material force. In "Man the Reformer" (January 25, 1841) he says, as the movement says, that the duty of each man is to be a "reformer." The "idea which now begins to agitate society has a wider scope than our daily employments, our households, and the institutions of property. We are to revise the whole of our social structure, the State, the school, religion, marriage, trade, science, and explore their foundations in our own nature.... What is a man born for but to be a Reformer, a Remaker of what man has made; a renouncer of lies; a restorer of truth and good.... If there are inconveniences and what is called ruin in the way, because we have so enervated and maimed ourselves, yet it would be like dying of perfumes to sink in the effort to re-attach the deeds of every day to the holy and mysterious recesses of life."[13] Emerson is reluctant to urge political activism. In "The Present Age" (February 23, 1837) he advocates verbal protest. He sees the dire need of putting on "asperities of individual character" and rising to speak out against decorum by unkempt speech, "tart tongue," plain and strong language by men who are "conscious each of such weight of character as absolve him from the yoke of etiquette and trifles." Individuals must cultivate the "higher faculties," throw off the yoke of decorous submission to the system, and be passionate in their protest.[14]

Nevertheless, we can trace a gradual deference to force in Emerson's essays. In "Self-Reliance" (March, 1841) he advocates non-conformity throughout society. "We want men and women who shall renovate life and our social state...." Political parties and conventions, however, weaken individuals. "It is

only as a man puts off all foreign support and stands alone that I see him to be strong and to prevail."[15] Only individuals of character can bring about social change. In "Man the Reformer" he recognizes that the self-reliant reformer cannot go alone; he has an obligation to "make it easier for all who follow." If need be, he must do more than "call the institutions of society to account;" he must be prepared to renounce his place in civilization, to go without, to return to the farm, to make a "hearty contribution of our energies to the common benefit; and we must not cease to tend to the correction of flagrant wrongs, by laying one stone aright every day." Revising the social structure will come through hope and faith, reliance on principles of character, kindness and love.[16] He does not advocate direct action other than by speech and self-removal. In "Lecture on the Times" (December 2, 1841) he takes a step closer to the position of the movement. He sympathizes with the "movement party" of his day. He calls the separate reform efforts all part of one movement; reformers are noble dissenters, aspirants, and theorists. He still rejects activism. The "soul of reform" is belief in man, in private character; it is the conviction that "reliance on the sentiment of man...will work best the more it is trusted." We need "new infusions of the spirit;" we want men, not actions.[17] In "The Transcendentalist" (January, 1842) he is less sympathetic than ever with activists. In "The Conservative" (December 9, 1841) he gives vigorous definition to the two "antagonistic" forces of society, conservatism and change, which emerge as political parties. The former is mean, holds fast, sits defensively on its "establishment" and saddles itself "with the mountainous load of the violence and vice of society, must deny the possibility of good, deny ideas, and suspect and stone the prophet.... Conservatism tends to universal seeming and treachery." Reform stands for openness, youth, hope, freedom, fulfillment, and change as the essential condition of life. He does not, however, side with the latter but takes a moderate, balanced position between the two.[18] In "The Young American" (February 7, 1844) he sounds more activist than conservative when he praises "beneficent socialism" and recognizes the good that private and public groups can do when they work for social reform. He is very specific. He argues that the duty of government is to spread general justice and humanity by educating the people and feeding the poor.[19] "New England Reformers" (March 3, 1844) carries activism still farther, for he recognizes that noisy protest and even some destruction of the old system are sometimes appropriate. He also concedes that if violence is dictated by the genius of the movement and is inevitable, not merely copied or the result of a mob frenzy, then it too is good. He is still committed to inner reform, however, rather than to activism, because reform, he says, is vitiated by partiality to specific reforms and by reliance on associations.[20] In the same year his pleasure at emancipation in the West Indies brought out his most vigorous endorsement of activism to date. He urged citizens to petition the legislature of his state to acknowledge the rights of slaves to be free.[21] On the occasion of the fourth anniversary of Webster's compromise speech of March 4, 1850, Emerson urged people to join the Anti-Slavery Society. He not only encouraged his wife's plan to drape their front gate with black but assisted friends "in the Concord Committee of correspondence" which helped lead the way to the liberal reform Republican party.[22] Another practical situation, John Brown's abortive raid at Harper's Ferry, spurred him to approve "the doctrine of armed resistance to the slavery men on the frontier." He "championed" Brown's cause and supported the war for abolition.[23] By this time he was almost 60 and was part of the establishment. It had taken specific events to bend his theories to activism.

I do not wish to give the impression that Emerson ever became a flaming radical. I agree with Rusk that he remained a staunch individualist and idealist. He is no "poet-laureate" of social revolution.[24] The extreme attitudes that he took during moments of crisis make him sound more radical than he was. He only sporadically espoused political activism. His Conduct of Life, published in 1860, strangely ignored the coming war and minimized the general injustices of the time. He was a liberal, a middle-of-the-roader. And liberalism is anathema to the movement. His revolutionary thought was that men be rugged individualists and that social reform would follow character reform. At a happening for the cult of youth, he would be equally out of place. He was already over thirty when he wrote the essays cited above. Although he grew a partial beard and smoked occasional cigars, he rejected pot and most stimulants. He ignored sex. He was timid about free speech, even though he advocated rudeness and boldness. He partly retracted his early praise of Whitman's poetry, and he advised against Whitman's publishing the "Children of Adam" sex poems in 1860.[25] By the movement's standards, Emerson was a hypocrite. He never martyred himself in the streets to the self-reliance of his teaching--only in the pulpit. Students find his rationalizations for inaction in the "Ode" highly offensive. Moreover, he praised the eternal, not the relevant. He was an idealist, a liberal; they are materialists and radicals.

Still, we have chalked up much that links Emerson to the tradition of the movement. He was aware of the generation gap. He understood the alienation of youth from a system that operates against self-

fulfillment. He understood their frustration. His analysis of the system that enslaves while it satisfies basic needs, his description of the antagonistic forces of society, and his definition of the mechanics of repression put him with Marx and Marcuse and the black revolutionaries. Emerson was arrogant like youth, and just as outspoken and antiestablishment. Most youth reject him, but he is one of their intellectual god-fathers.

Furman University

1 "Self-Reliance," Essays: First Series (The Complete Works of Ralph Waldo Emerson, edited by Edward Waldo Emerson, Centenary Edition) (Boston: Houghton Mifflin Company, 1903), II, 49-50. This edition is hereafter cited as CW.
2 Jack Newfield, A Prophetic Minority (New York: New American Library, 1967), pp. 90, 24, 150-151.
3 "Lecture on the Times," Nature, Addresses and Lectures, CW, I, 260.
4 "The Young American," CW, I, 388.
5 "The Present Age," The Early Lectures of Ralph Waldo Emerson, 2 vols. (Cambridge: Harvard University Press, 1964), II, 158-159, 169, 157-162 passim.
6 "The Conservative," CW, I, 306, 307-309ff. 7 "The Present Age," Early Lectures, II, 158.
8 "The Conservative," CW, I, 260. 9 "The Young American," CW, I, 387.
10 Herbert Marcuse, One-Dimensional Man: Studies in the Ideology of Advanced Industrial Society (Boston: Beacon Press, 1964), pp. 4-5, 7-8, 11, 13-14, 51-52 and elsewhere.
11 "The Present Age," Early Lectures, II, 160, 161-163. 12 Marcuse, pp. 7, 250-257.
13 CW, I, 247-248. 14 Early Lectures, II, 161, 162. 15 CW, II, 75, 89.
16 CW, I, 228, 243, 247-252. 17 CW, I, 268, 276, 281, 278. 18 CW, I, 297-298.
19 CW, I, 380-381, 384, 387. 20 Essays: Second Series, CW, III, 254, 260-263.
21 The Complete Essays and Other Writings of Ralph Waldo Emerson, Modern Library College Editions, Edited, with Biographical Introduction, by Brooks Atkinson (New York: The Modern Library, 1950), p. 849.
22 Ralph L. Rusk, The Life of Ralph Waldo Emerson (New York: Charles Scribner's Sons, 1949), p. 369.
23 Rusk, pp. 397, 402, 416. 24 Rusk, p. 371.
25 Rusk, p. 403. See also "The Poet," Essays: Second Series, CW, III, 27-29.

EMERSON'S "YOUNG AMERICAN" AS DEMOCRATIC NOBLEMAN

JOHN Q. ANDERSON

If some phrases in "The Young American" were translated into the rhetoric of the youth movements of the 1960's, Emerson might well be considered a prophet by the under-thirty generation. He attacks social status based on the accumulation of material goods; he criticizes traditional education and advocates educational opportunities for the poor; he defends the weak; he urges sensitive young people to flee the cities to the more wholesome countryside; and he speaks approvingly of "beneficent socialism" and imagines a society based on "love and labor." But parallels between Emerson's criticism of society in his time and social protest movements in the 1960's are more apparent than real. Revolutionary as he appeared to his own time, Emerson was well within the Christian and humanistic tradition, so much so that his insistence on self-discipline and responsible individualism and his opposition to organized reform movements

would instantly mark him as "establishment." On the other hand, Emerson's ideas might well offer a pattern for the 1970's, if young people were willing to accept the rigorous individual reform that he advocated.

"The Young American" was delivered as a lecture before the Mercantile Library Association in Boston on February 7, 1844, and a revised version of it was published in The Dial shortly thereafter.[1] Those who heard the lecture or who read the essay could easily have mistaken his words for another of the many contemporary tributes to "Manifest Destiny,"[2] because of Emerson's favorable attitude toward the expansion of railroads and his praise of trade and commerce. But careful reading of the lecture reveals that Emerson was not echoing the sentiments of newspapers and politicians who were agitating for extending the national boundaries to the Pacific ocean. Instead, he was appealing to sensitive young people of that time to take advantage of the material progress of the youthful nation and to build on it a society that would be "a new and more excellent social state than history has recorded" (Works, I, 395).[3]

"The Young American" was written during the period of Emerson's greatest enthusiasm for America as "the home of man," a place where man could at last develop the full potential so long promised. Also, he was at the time most actively seeking for evidence of American "genius," especially "the poet" who could, as he said in the essay bearing that name, use "our incomparable materials" (III, 37). He was especially concerned about the young men who, as he had said about his own generation, "were born with knives in their brain, a tendency to introversion, self-dissection, anatomizing of motives" (X, 329). Forty-one years old when he read the lecture, Emerson remembered what it was like to be young and sensitive in "hasty, facile America," in "this unpoetic American forest" (Journals, V, 241),[4] where the dominant materialism smothered the creative spirit; he knew the temptation to escape to the more congenial atmosphere of Europe, as he himself had done barely ten years before only to find it an illusion, concluding that Americans had listened too long to the siren song of the old world.[5] Behind the facade of European culture, particularly in England, lingered vestiges of feudalism, social concepts that conflicted with the American belief in individual freedom. Thus, he said in the introduction to his lecture, "our people have their intellectual culture from one country and their duties from another. This false state of things," he asserted, "is newly in a way to be corrected" (365). The remainder of the lecture shows how this change would be effected.

Taking his usual long view, Emerson envisioned the emergence of a national spirit that would diminish the influence of Europe. This evolution would have three phases: first, the railroads that were rapidly uniting the far-flung areas of the nation would ultimately produce a new sense of national unity; second, trade and commerce--anti-feudal and thus anti-European--would further strengthen the trend toward national self-confidence; and, third, land, readily accessible because of the new modes of transportation, would exert a "sanative" influence on the people and thereby reinforce the growing feeling of unity and self-confidence. These forces, aided by the ameliorating tendency of the "beneficent destiny," would ultimately lead to an "American sentiment," a spirit of true nationalism that would enable Americans to stand unashamed before the world.

Having established these three points, he proceeded to elaborate upon them, one at a time. His enthusiasm for railroad expansion may well have astounded those in his audience who had expected him to discuss more transcendental ideas. Railroads, Emerson contended, overcame the problem of distance which had been a deterrent to the unified feeling necessary in politics and trade. "Railroad iron," he said, "is a magician's rod, in its power to evoke the sleeping energies" of the nation (364). Easier travel and transportation of goods eliminate old barriers of national descent, occupational differences, and regional prejudices to promote cohesion. This "unlooked-for consequence of the railroad" had further acquainted Americans with "the boundless resources of their own soil." As a result, "The bountiful continent, state on state, territory on territory, to the waves of the Pacific" demanded a correspondingly expansive national consciousness. Further, this feeling was the unforeseen outgrowth of the purely trading spirit that in the beginning had established colonies on the Atlantic shores of the continent.

Significant as railroad expansion was, Emerson felt that the most important fact in America in 1844 was the continuing rise of commerce. In the early history of the nation, trade brought wealth and power to the traders and thereby weakened European feudalism; in that sense, it worked by indirect means for the ultimate benefit of man on this continent. Trade as a new agent in the world had progressed from initial physical strength necessary to voyages to an intellectual phase of computation, combination, and information. "Trade," he claimed, "[is] a plant which grows wherever there is peace, as soon as there is peace,

and as long as there is peace" (377). Trade did not establish a new kind of aristocracy to replace the feudal sort; being impermanent, it rises and falls and is an instrument in the hands of the beneficent destiny which works for the ultimate good of all. By the natural process of change, the ascendency of trade and commerce in America is bound to give way to something new, for trade has its limitations; it eventually puts all on the market--talent, beauty, virtue, and man himself.

Meanwhile, land--the third element in Emerson's vision for the future--"is the appointed remedy for whatever is false and fantastic in our culture." Whereas the ownership of land in Europe had been limited largely to the upperclass, in America any man could own it, and the railroads were placing it within the reach of all. Land, Emerson contended, repairs "the errors of a scholastic and traditional education and brings us into just relations with men and things" (366). Unlike business, trade, and commerce, agriculture is an area that is not crowded, and the farmer, unlike the business man, is independent of markets. More importantly, the moral benefits derived from tilling the soil--the sanative influence--result in improvement of the land and the nation as well. The availability of land, Emerson argued, invites agriculture, gardening, and domestic architecture. America had yet to learn the European art of cultivating public gardens for the general good. The beauty of nature, even as arranged by man, increases public appreciation of beauty generally and indirectly contributes to the "American sentiment." Beautifying the land through establishing parks and private estates was the one fine art left to Americans, "now that sculpture, painting, and religious and civil architecture have become effete" in Europe and in imitative American cities. Since a beautiful garden or estate makes "it indifferent where one lives," Americans have the opportunity of enjoying the sanative influence of the soil at a distance from cities, because the railroads have made travel easy.

Although in the past the American cities had enticed young people away from the country, the trend had been reversed, Emerson believed; even more of them now would leave the cities for the greater freedom and inspiration of nature in the country. This movement "will further the most poetic of all occupations of real life," he declared, bringing out the hidden graces of the landscape. The fact that most Americans then lived by the land showed its influence upon the development of the nation and indicated future developments. Again, the railroads that provided easier transportation would diminish the influence of the eastern seaboard. The "nervous, rocky West" was thrusting a continental element into the national consciousness. "We cannot look on the freedom of this country, in connexion with its youth, without presentiment that here shall laws and institutions exist on a scale of proportion to the majesty of nature." "To men legislating for the area betwixt the two oceans, betwixt the snows and the tropics, somewhat of the gravity of nature will infuse itself into the code" (370). People drawn from all over the world would contribute their work, their voice, and their thought so that ultimately America would become more representative of mankind--"the country of the Future"; "it is a country of beginnings, of projects, of designs, of expectations" because "there is a sublime and friendly Destiny by which the human race is guided, --the race never dying, the individual never spared, --to results affecting masses and ages" (371). This "Destiny" is infused into nature where it operates by amelioration--shaping, changing, balancing.[6] Becuase it works for the masses of men, it is a "terrible communist, reserving all profits to the community without dividends to the individual" (373). Consequently, those who promote the development of the nation--the builders of railroads, colleges, hospitals and makers of laws--derive the smallest benefits from their work, the largest accruing to future generations. But the individual is not lost in this ameliorating tendency of Destiny; what benefits the masses also benefits him. Convinced that trade, then at its height in America, would eventually be replaced by inevitable change, he admitted that he could not clearly foresee what would replace it beyond two important trends--beneficent socialism and expansion of education.

Beneficent socialism, then a considerable movement in France, Germany, Switzerland, and England, was also evident in America.[7] Leaders in this movement desired a greater freedom for man from the traditionalism of the past. They felt that government was not providing for the basic needs of the people--education, work, and guidance. The preferred way of life for these communalists was agrarian, but not the old agriculture with its toil and neglect of individual needs. A strong point in this movement, he believed, was the insistence on a thorough and equal education. Work on the land combined with education would make the best use of the sanative influence of the land and of nature. Founded on love and labor, communal associations proposed to substitute harmonious industry for hostile competition, though objections to them had been raised. For one thing, they paid for talent and labor at the same rate, not recognizing that "the value of money lies in knowing what to do with it" (383). Also, mothers of families objected that communal living was

less desirable than the privacy of family life in the older pattern. Even so, the communal associations had shown that experimentation in social change was possible and that even greater social evolution was on the way. But the national government must be alert to this inevitable social change. So far "Government has been a fossil; it should be a plant" (379). "We have a feudal government in a commercial age," he said. For one thing, education should be available for poor people, because education could be the means whereby they are enabled to rise to the heights of their talents. Furthermore, government should provide guidance for all citizens in order to give them a chance to employ their talents. Nature provides men who are born leaders and advisers, and education and guidance of the right kind, provided by government, would enable them to find their right places. "In every society," he observed, "some men are born to rule and some to advise." Let the powers be directed by love and "they would everywhere be greeted with joy and honor."

"I call upon you, young men," Emerson said, "to obey your heart and be the nobility of this land."[8] The remainder of the essay explains the special kind of "nobility" he meant. Obviously with European aristocracy in mind, he warned young men that their role would not be "to drink wine and ride in a fine coach," but rather "to guide and adorn life for the multitude by forethought, by elegant studies, by perseverance, self-devotion, and the remembrance of the humble old friend," and by making their lives "secretly beautiful" (387). Every age of the world has produced a leading nation, he added, "one of a more generous sentiment, whose eminent citizens were willing to stand for the interest of general justice and humanity, at the risk of being called, by the men of the moment, chimerical and fantastic." "Which," he asked, "should be that nation but these States? Which should lead that movement, if not New England? Who should lead the leaders, but the Young American?" (387-388). He then charged Young Americans with the creation of a "high national feeling," missing from those "organs...presumed to speak a popular sense"--"our state papers or legislative debate," lyceums, churches, and newspapers, which "recommend conventional virtues, whatever will earn and preserve property." They were to cultivate the "private mind," which "has access to the totality of goodness and truth that it may be a balance to a corrupt society; and to stand for the private verdict against popular clamor...." As the nation's "noble men," they were to develop the "noble mind." That justice might be done, they were "to throw [themselves] on the side of weakness, of youth, of hope; on the liberal, on the expansive side, never on the defensive, the conserving, the timorous, the lock-and-bolt system" (388-390).

Aware that the day had not arrived for wide acceptance of his views, he admitted that the American "public mind wants self-respect." "We are full of vanity, of which the most signal proof is our sensitiveness to foreign and especially English censure" (392). He blamed this timidity on the American habit of "immense reading" of the "productions of the English press." He conceded that "to imaginative persons in this country there is somewhat bare and bald in our short history and unsettled wilderness. They ask, who would live in a new country that can live in an old? and is it not strange that our youths and maidens should burn to see the picturesque extremes of an antiquated country?" (392). But, he warns, it is one thing to visit a country and another to live there. Appealing as the surface manners and ceremonies of English aristocracy might be, an American would resent the restraints. Emerson could see no justice in a system in which "no man of letters, be his eminence what it may, is received into the best society, except as a lion and a show" (394). He ended his lecture with this impassioned plea: "Let us live in America, too thankful for our want of feudal institutions...youth is a fault of which we shall daily mend. This land too is as old as the Flood, and wants no ornament or privilege which nature could bestow.... If only the men are employed in conspiring with the designs of the Spirit who led us hither and is leading us still, we shall quickly enough advance out of all hearing of others' censures, out of all regrets of our own, into a new and more excellent social state than history has recorded (394-395). The audience that winter evening in Boston in 1844 well knew that what they had heard had little relationship to the journalists' and politicians' "Manifest Destiny." Those who had read "Self-Reliance" when it appeared three years before recognized the parallels, and young men in the audience doubtless experienced some of the same exhilaration. "The Young American" is much more specific in criticism of the American government and in suggesting to youth its place in society. It is a practical application of the principles of responsible individualism expressed in "Self-Reliance." It appeals to youth to change the dominant pattern of materialism, urging a "revolution" within the establishment, not a destruction of it. Emerson firmly believed that if society were ever to be improved, reform must begin with the individual, and he himself had gone a long way down that road before he wrote those audacious statements in "Self-Reliance." If many individuals followed this pattern of self-improvement, then society would in the end be transformed; thus Emerson places the responsibility squarely on the individual, not on "the establishment," "the government," or some vague "they," as is so often the case

in our time. Read as Emerson intended, "The Young American" could become meaningful to youth in the 1970's: individuals acquire "rights" only when they accept responsibility, and responsibility means self-discipline. Cultivation of the "private mind" to an understanding of the "totality of goodness and truth," as he put it, might yet produce the "noble mind" of "noble men"--Emerson's democratic noblemen.

University of Houston

1 In his notes to the essay (Works, I, 451-455), E. W. Emerson prints two passages, originally appearing in the April, 1844, number of The Dial, but omitted when Emerson included the lectures in Miscellanies.
2 See John Q. Anderson, "Emerson and 'Manifest Destiny,'" Boston Public Library Quarterly, VII (Jan., 1955), 23-33.
3 The Complete Works of Ralph Waldo Emerson, ed. Edward Waldo Emerson (Boston: Houghton Mifflin Co., 1903-1904); hereafter cited throughout the text. With the exception of one reference to Emerson's Journals, all parentheses refer to the Works, the solitary page numbers referring to volume one.
4 The Journals of Ralph Waldo Emerson, ed. Edward Waldo Emerson and Waldo Emerson Forbes (Boston: Houghton Mifflin Co., 1909-1914).
5 Philip L. Nicoloff, Emerson on Race and History: An Examination of English Traits (N.Y.: Columbia University Press, 1961) says (p. 12) that Emerson adopted from his father the dictum that the influence of Europe, mainly England, was fatal to American genius. American freedom "from bondage to foreign cultures--especially from the English culture--became a fundamental ingredient of his program" (p. 20).
6 Nicoloff (p. 115) thinks that the reading of Robert Chambers' Vestiges of Creation in 1843 was influential on Emerson's concept of amelioration.
7 Bernard Cohen, "Emerson's 'The Young American' and Hawthorne's 'The Intelligence Office,'" American Literature, XXVI (March, 1954), 32-43, points out that Emerson's conversations with Hawthorne during the time the lecture was being written produced several strands of thought that appear in the essay, particularly the commentary on the community experiments.
8 John G. Cawelti, Apostles of the Self-Made Man (Chicago: University of Chicago Press, 1965), p. 93, says, "Emerson believed, as Jefferson did, that most aristocracies were artificial.... The natural aristocracy is constituted largely of self-made men, too busy making their way to become 'society's gentlemen.'"

EMERSON'S METHOD AS A PHILOSOPHER

WILLIAM B. BARTON

"...the face of Nature remains irresistibly alluring."[1]

The problems of the unity, goal, style and logic of Emerson's thought are inseparably bound up with the one question of method. Although different strains of his thinking, like that of any widely read author, are traceable to certain sources, each becomes Emerson's after passing through his original mind. The method he adopts as a means of ordering human experience philosophically is no exception: the method of Natural Philosophy. The following discussion deals with the sources of Emerson's method, the evolution of its principles, and some of its applications. Finally, I will briefly comment on the relevance of his philosophy for our time.

I.

Three events in Emerson's life are important in the development of his method. A journal entry of July 13, 1833, details his feelings while viewing Jussieu's Cabinets in Paris at the Jardin des Plantes, when,

moved by "strange sympathies," he found himself continually repeating, "I will be a naturalist."[2] A few months before this experience, when still wrestling with his soul as pastor of the Second Church in Boston, he hunted in "Charles' dish of shells each new form of beauty and new tint," supposing that "an entire cabinet of shells would be an expression of the whole human mind" (J, IV, 13-14). Fourteen years later, on the occasion of his second European visit, he reminded a London audience how one could be surprised with "occult sympathies" on going through the British Museum, Jardin des Plantes, "or any cabinet where is some representation of all the kingdoms of Nature" (W, XII, 22). This lecture with two others given at the same time[3] were later published under their original title, The Natural History of the Intellect. This theme, repeated often in later years, was chosen finally for a kind of summing-up of his life's work and delivered at Harvard (1870), and again the following year with some deletions and additions.[4]

The choice of "The Uses of Natural History" for the topic of his very first lecture (November 4 [6], 1833)[5] in a series of four on Science, was not a popularizing attempt at displaying ability for speaking on any subject after a suitable time for reading up on it (the habit of many Lyceum speakers), but the result of a profound commitment to a new method, which had grown out of his own reading, reflection, and experience. He proceeded with at least as much seriousness in applying this method as did Descartes in his methodic search for clear and distinct ideas developing his thought with as much strictness as the media of public lectures and writing, and the limits of the method itself, permitted. We find in 1833 the pronouncement of the fundamental Emersonian point of departure: "For, every form is a history of the thing" (EL, I, 17).

This article of philosphic faith had probably evolved from his reflections on Goethe's proposition that "Nature...became the tell-tale of her own secrets"[6] as well as from his own experience. It became the basic premise in his application of the method of Natural History. He had read and thought long on Coleridge's essays in The Friend (J, IV, 290), in addition to Goethe's Metamorphose der Pflanzen (EL, I, 79).[7] Sherman Paul has shown the importance of these two works for the theory of correspondence of the moral and physical worlds--Emerson's answer to both Lockean and Humean empiricism.[8] But one can be too eager to see likenesses between the Englishman, the German, and Emerson, while failing to see the ways in which the American moves beyond both. If one suggests that Emerson was not concerned with the "subtle distinctions of philosophical thought" or that he "seized from the past speculation about the nature of man and the universe any idea that pointed in the direction of their correspondence,"[9] he does him an injustice. This oversimplification portrays him as proceeding haphazardly rather than in any serious philosophical way. The scrap-book view of Emerson's method of philosophizing has held the field too long; unfortunately it is a difficult misconception to correct. Emerson's strength lies, first of all, in realizing the need of a sound method and then in applying it to the whole of human experience. Despite all this, we are frequently left with a view of Emerson which he reserved for Bacon, who did not arrange facts but only unceasingly collected them. "All his work is therefore somewhat fragmentary. The fire has hardly passed over it and given it fusion and a new order from his own mind.... [Bacon's was] the order of a shop and not that of a tree or an animal where perfect assimilation has taken place and all the parts have a perfect unity" (EL, I, 334-335).

Emerson's search for a "natural" rather than an "arbitrary" Classification, along with the fact that he found "no Method philosophical in any one" of the natural sciences of his time (J, IV, 288), made him responsive to certain suggestions in Coleridge, whose insistence upon "initiative," i.e., the habit of foreseeing the whole in each integral part, was especially attractive. It entailed the "progressive transition," or "transition with continuity," from one part of an arrangement to another, but always with a "preconception" or "Idea" (J, IV, 287) as the guiding principle in mind--best illustrated in his analysis of Shakespeare's characters, since "in them all we still feel ourselves communing with the same nature, which is everywhere present as the vegetable sap in the sprays, leaves, buds, blossoms, and fruits, their shapes, taste and colors."[10] Emerson must have readily agreed with the opinion of Coleridge about the chaotic state of zoology as a mere assemblage of disconnected facts and phenomena before John Hunter (one of the first great modern Naturalists) seized upon the unifying idea of comparative studies and proceeded to construct his museum "for the scientific apprehension out of the unspoken alphabet of nature."[11]

Another profound influence on Emerson was Goethe, who summarized once the argument of his Metamorphosis of Plants in some poetic lines, written apparently to aid his wife, who seems to have been somewhat discouraged by the classifying names of the prevailing system of Linneaus: "The rich profusion

thee confounds, my love, / Of flowers, spread athwart the garden. Aye, / Name upon name assails thy ears, and each / More barbarous-sounding than the one before."[12] But out of the confusion comes a hint of some secret connection between the differing forms, wherein the earlier gives rise to the later, the history of the plant being read in the leaf and fruit.

> Ah, love could I vouchsafe
> In sweet felicity a simple answer!
> Gaze on them as they grow, see how the plant
> Burgeons by stages into flower and fruit,
> . . . .
> The infinite freedom of the growing leaf.

How successful Goethe was in clarifying biological principles of classification on this occasion, we do not know; but his work anticipated Darwin and sparked the imagination of young Emerson, confirming his belief in the principle which he generalized into a philosophical axiom: "Every form is a history of the thing." Whereas Goethe had read the history of the plant in the transformations of the leaf, Emerson saw the brother of man's hand "even now cleaving the Arctic Sea in the fin of the whale, and, innumerable ages since, was pawing the marsh in the flipper of the saurus" (EL, I, 32). Furthermore, he not only anticipates Darwin[13] but seems also to have appreciated the place of environmental factors in survival. "There was a time," he asserts in his second lecture, "The Relation of Man to the Globe" (1833), "when the creatures of one sort had reached that number that it became necessary to check their multiplication; or, by their habits, had wrought such changes on the surface of the globe, as to make the earth habitable in a finer and more complex creation" (EL, I, 31).

In 1836, the year Darwin returned from the voyage of the *H.M.S. Beagle*, Emerson published *Nature* in which he reached his own evolutionary philosophy: "In a cabinet of natural history," he writes recalling his visit to the Jardin des Plantes, "we become sensible of a certain occult recognition and sympathy in regard to the most unwieldy and eccentric forms of beast, fish, and insect.... Nor has science sufficient humanity, so long as the naturalist overlooks that wonderful congruity which subsists between man and the world; of which he is lord, not because he is the most subtile inhabitant, but because he is its head and heart, and finds something of himself in every great and small thing, in every mountain stratum, in every new law of color, fact of astronomy, or atmospheric influence which observation or analysis lays open" (W, I, 67-68).

Five years, in fact, before Darwin's paper was published in the Linnaean Society in 1858, Emerson read an essay on *Poetry* to a small company in M. D. Conway's room in Cambridge.[14] Much of it appeared (1883) in *Letters and Social Aims* (W, VIII, 1-19). Here his evolutionary thought, which he generalizes in a fundamental principle of all Nature to account for the appearance of man, is clearly stated. He refers to John Hunter's *arrested and progressive development*, which indicated "the way upward from the invisible protoplasm to the highest organisms,--gave the poetic key to natural science." Among the Naturalists he mentions Goethe, Agassiz, and [Erasmus] Darwin, whose theories hint of a power "not yet exhausted, showing unity and perfect order in physics." Furthermore, the most skeptical chemist and analyzer "scornful of all but the driest fact is forced to keep the poetic curve of Nature.... Anatomy, osteology, exhibit arrested and progressive ascent in each kind, the lower pointing to the higher forms, the higher to the highest, from the fluid in an elastic sack, from radiate, mollusk, articulate, vertebrate, up to man; as if the whole animal world were only a Hunterian museum to exhibit the genesis of mankind" (W, VIII, 7-8).

Emerson, in fact, was among the first modern philosophers to set forth the outlines of a thoroughgoing process philosophy of organism founded on evolutionary principles. In its ontological implications it is at least as imposing as Bergson or Whitehead, although his orientation is that of poet rather than scientist or philosopher of science. In his lecture on "The Naturalist" he tells his audience, "I fully believe in both, in the poetry and in the dissection" EL, I, 79). His philosophical development would not have been enhanced one bit by some original contribution to the natural sciences. His strength lay in generalizing the method of Natural History and applying it to the whole of human experience. This reminds us of Whitehead's "synoptic vision" gained through the method of "imaginative generalization."[15] Believing there is "no false logic in Nature" (EL, I, 75), Emerson's interest in Natural History, therefore, was not a demand of popular oratory but the expression of profound conviction, a guiding thought throughout his life: "for so much of nature as he [man] is ignorant of, just so much of his own mind does he not yet possess" (EL, II, 34). Having noted the more important of the sources of Emerson's method, we look next at the evolution of its principles. There are seven points of interest.

II.

1. A Natural Method. Emerson was impressed with Jussieu's natural method of classification over the more arbitrary and artificial Linnaeus. He listened in Paris to the son of the famous author of Genera plantarum. When published in 1789, this work set botany and the whole of Natural History on a new path.[16] "The Garden itself," he noted in his journal, "is admirably arranged. They have attempted to classify all the plants in the ground, to put together, that is as nearly as may be the conspicuous plants of each class on Jussieu's system" (J, IV, 198-200). His experience at viewing this particular collection was decisive in the development of his own method. The next year his lecture The Naturalist, (1833) further illustrated the significance of that experience. He told his audience, "no intelligent person can come into a well arranged cabinet of natural productions, without being excited to unusual reveries, without being conscious by instinctive perception of relations which he can only feel without being able to comprehend or define" (EL, I, 81-82, italics mine).

2. Rejection of the analytic method. Emerson, like Bergson later, rejected the method of arbitrary definition and analysis which destroyed the unity and natural relationships of a being. He asked a Boston audience (1833) about "The Method of Nature: Who could ever analyze it? That rushing stream will not stop to be observed. We can never surprise nature in a corner; never find the end of a thread; never tell where to set the first stone" (W, I, 199).

Years later (1870), he told his young Harvard audience that analysis leaves one "as far from the Being," as a boy who breaks his drum to find out what makes the noise. "T'is the wrong path. For fruit, for wisdom, for power, these things must be used, not-spied." He deplored the approach to Nature of a "detective." "I am not anatomist. I see and wonder."[17] He had suggested a similar thought to a London audience the first time he lectured on "The Natural History of the Intellect" (1848): Analysis "is cold and bereaving and, shall I say it? somewhat spying" (W, XII, 14).

3. Must not look for completeness. He did not think it possible to expect completeness in one's view of things. The universe is open and changing. "I write metaphysics, but my method is purely expectant. It is not even tentative." Skeptical of any attempt at completeness and finality, he likened such presumption to a gnat attempting to grasp the world. The metaphysicians manage to draw only "jejune outlines." "My attention, my love, can only be commanded by the single aperçus. I think we must not presume wholeness, be content with as many particular insights they [the metaphysicians] have, and with only a sketch of the whole."[18]

He was impressed with the processes of Nature, the openness of each of its operations, the spontaneity and changes which surprise the man prepared to receive them with new revelations everyday. Man must identify with this unpredictable side of things. "Nature halts calculators; her methods are saltatory and impulsive. Man lives by pulses; our organic movements are such; and the chemical and etheral agents are undulatory and alternate; and the mind goes antagonizing on, and never prospers but by fits.... In the thought of genius there is always a surprise" (W, III, 68).

4. Classification. Classification is natural where its objects are arranged as they are first given to us, "containing their own reason in themselves, and making known facts continually" (J, IV, 289). Only in this way does the true Idea behind Nature become accessible to the philosopher or the poet who would speak of it. "This it is to conceive of acts and works, to throw myself into the object so that its history shall naturally evolve itself before me. Well so does the Universe, Time, History, evolve itself, so simply, so unmiraculously from the All Perceiving Mind" (J, IV, 285, italics mine). Classification, therefore, apart from Reason, or the attempt to unify under an idea, would be empty. But he rejects accepting any classification as absolute and immutable "but merely as full of tendency" (J, IV, 290).

5. Composition. To see things as much as possible within their natural setting; to compose one's philosophical cabinet where true relationships are left untouched and where deeper ties are disclosed; to see the root affinity of all things, each to each and each to man--this was a lesson apparently which he learned while still a boy and which became as important in the development of his philosophy as had been Charles' cabinet of shells. "I remember when I was a boy going upon the beach and being charmed with the colors and forms of the shells. I picked up many and put them in my pocket. When I got home I could find nothing

that I gathered--nothing but some [old] dry ugly mussel and snail shells. Thence I learned that *composition was more important than the beauty of individual forms to effect*. On the shore they lay wet and social by the sea and under the sky" (J, IV, 291, italics mine). Things in composition give us insight into the "secret logic" of Nature, and the philosopher's task is to describe and report what he sees and hears always respecting the inner constitution of things. A basic interconnection of things, when brought under a unifying idea, even if it is just the temperature of the weather, will disclose meaning. "My notes, I find, are like the contributions of many a citizen who twice a day visits his thermometer, and so is able to furnish at last a faithful meterologic calendar of several years to the Coast Survey. Yet this is not quite useless to science, and mine is a list of farmers Almanac of mental moods."[19]

But one must learn to see things as a whole--to allow them to speak for themselves. At first they may be indistinguishable, but patience will produce results. One passage in the *Journals* reminds us of Husserl's phenomenological method of describing the immediate data of awareness: "At the centre it is a black spot--no line, no handle, no character; I am tempted to stray to the accessible lanes on the left hand and right, which lead round it--all outside of it. Intellectual courage, intellectual duty says we must not blink the question, we must march up to it and sit down [at] before it [the town] and watch there incessantly getting as close as we can to the black wall, and watch and watch, until slowly lines and handles and characters shall appear on its surface and we shall learn to open the gate and enter the fortress, un[cover] it and lay bare its ground plan...." (J, IV, 290).

6. *Insight*. True insight comes with an intuitive suddenness, if one has not violated the canons of nature in his approach to arrange, classify and understand her. So dawns in the mind the true Idea according to which the universe is made--as a surprise, as a flash. "...and yet in all the permutations and combinations supposable, might not a cabinet of shells or a flora be thrown into one which should flash on us the very thought" (J, IV, 288). "Life is a series of surprises, and would not be worth taking or keeping if it were not" (W, III, 67). He refers to this "surprise" and immediacy of insight in a passage resembling a K'oan in spirit: "I make: O no! I clap my hands in infantile joy and amazement before the first opening to me of this august magnificence, old with the love and homage of innumerable ages, young with the life of life, the sunbright Mecca of the desert" (W, III, 71-72).

This insight, therefore, comes only when one has assumed the proper attitude toward natural events--when one *sees*. "As I am, so I see" (W, III, 79). Teilhard de Chardin wrote, "...the whole of life lies in that verb--if not in end, at least in essence. Fuller being is closer union.... union can only increase through an increase in consciousness, that is to say in vision.... *To see or to perish* is the very condition laid upon everything that makes up the universe...."[20] Emerson would have found little to disagree with in the thought of this modern French philosopher-scientist, at least, on this point. In a letter to George Bush, he wrote: "It is my habit to assume always as purely as I can the attitude of an observer, and to record what I see.... But what I see now, --the feeblest intellection rightly considered, implies all the vast attributes of spirit, implies the uprising of the one divine soul into my particular creek and bay and apprises me that the ocean is behind. I think that the constant progress of the human mind is from observation of superficial differences to intrinsic analogues, and at last, to control identity, in all things. The εν και παν I everywhere behold."[21]

7. *Point of Departure*: *The Middle Region*. One begins his approach to Nature or Being, so far as philosophy is concerned, from the kind of average everyday understanding of things which is given in the very act of living. The "middle region of our being" is the "temperate zone." To wander in the "thin and cold realm of pure geometry and lifeless science, or sink into that of sensation" will not yield the great gifts of nature. It is the "narrow belt" between those two extremes; or as he puts it, "in popular experience everything good is on the highway" (W, III, 62). Having noticed the evolution of the basic principles of Emerson's method, we now survey its application in the clarification of the *unity*, *goal*, *style*, and *logic* of his philosophy.

III.

1. *Unity*. In 1884, just two years after Emerson's death, the brilliant St. Louis Hegelian, W. T. Harris, wrote an answer to the charge that the *Essays* were "a vast number of brilliant statements, loosely connected and bound into paragraphs, with only such unity as is given by the lids of the volume." He argued for a *dialectic unity* in Emerson's prose, *i.e.*, "an unfolding of the subject according to its natural growth

in experience;" the object of Emerson's writing being not to make proselytes but "to present truth and to produce insight...."[22] Harris did not seem to appreciate fully that Emerson thought himself to have already moved a step beyond Hegel, whom he classified with the abstract metaphysicians. "I know what step Berkeley took, and recognize the same in the Hindoo books. Hegel took a second.... But is there not room for a third step? There is not room for many steps. It needs not any Encyclopaedia of volumes to tell."[23] A cold abstract metaphysical system gave only an artificial unity, which, for Emerson, Hegel's own Encyclopaedia personified. But what was Emerson's "third step"? It was his insight into Reality as a process organically arranged and evolving, where each entity shows something of the life of every other one and each participating in and identical with the Divine Intellect. Such a position asserts the organic unity of the whole at any one moment--not some far-off achievable moment at the consummation of history.

Emerson never flinched from his basic faith in the ultimate organic unity of the world, which incorporates all differences without destroying them. This faith was still present in his Harvard lecture on "Identity" (May 19, 1870): "I do not know that I should feel threatened or insulted if the chemist should take his protoplasm or should mix his hydrogen, oxygen and carbon and make a plant or animalcule incontestably swimming and jumping before my eyes. I might feel that the day had arrived when the human race might be trusted with a new device of power, and its immense responsibility; for these steps are not solitary or local, but give only a hint of an advancing frontier supported by an advancing race behind it."[24]

In the "Transcendency of Physics," another lecture in the same series, he asserts, "The world may be reeled off from any one of its laws like a ball of yarn."[25] He was convinced of the fundamental unity of all things and that the "wildest variety of form and function explains itself as gradating of one harmonious whole."[26] Again, "we say, man in Nature; we find later, that we may also say, Nature in man. The miracle of the world is the tally of things to thought."[27]

2. Goal. Emerson had early set himself the task of working out the Natural History of the Intellect. Impressed with the success of the method of Natural History and once rid of its artificiality, in chemistry and botany, he wondered whether it might be applied to "a higher class of facts; to those laws, namely, which are common to chemistry, anatomy, astronomy, geometry, intellect, morals and social life;--laws of the world?" (W, XII, 3-4)--"the powers and laws of the Intellect." This task became his life-time goal. Intellect becomes symbolic for the life of the world. Thirty-seven years (1870) after his first lecture on "The Uses of Natural History" (1833), he summed up the attraction the subject had sustained for him in that "its grasp is immense." Nothing falls beyond its realm, "not a science, not an art, not a trade, not a word of man, speech of orator, hymn of poet, prayer of priest, witticism at table, but this sets us on the analysis to find wherein the power, wisdom, worth, or fun lies,--no anecdote and no act of earnest or of play that does not interest us as students of the mind."[28] I cannot agree with those who say Emerson failed to carry through this task. The comprehensiveness of his thought, incorporating, as it does, insight from both Eastern and Western traditions, as well as his view of Intellect as transcending the subject-object dichotomy, places his interests and emphasis in philosophy more in keeping with those of the twentieth century.

3. Style. (A) Language. The influence of the method of Natural History on Emerson's style is grasped in the notion of the origin and function of language. It is first clearly discussed in Nature (1836): "Words are signs of natural facts. The use of natural history is to give us aid in supernatural history" (W, I, 25), i.e., mental terms if traced to their origin invariably designate some natural fact. The term right originally meant straight; transgression, the crossing of a line, etc. Children and savages give us a clue as to the process in which this analogy came about, since they "use only nouns or names of things, which they convert into verbs, and apply to analogous mental acts" (W, I, 26). Back of his theory is the belief in natural facts as symbolic of mental facts; thus natural appearances correspond to states of the mind, which are describable only "by presenting that natural appearance as its picture" (W, I, 26).

Emerson is not concerned with cataloging facts; it is the relationship between Nature and man which enables man to draw analogies. Man in relation to all things and the relation of all things to him become the bases for his positing Reason or Intellect as the warp and woof of all, the matrix out of which both man and Nature arise. Thus, "All the facts in natural history taken by themselves, have no value, but are barren like a single sex. But marry it to human history, and it is full of life. Whole floras, all Linnaeus' and Buffon's volumes, are dry catalogues of facts; but the most trivial of these facts, the habit of a plant, the organs, or work, or noise of an insect, applied to the illustration of a fact in intellectual philosophy, or in any way associated to human nature, affects us in the most lively and agreeable manner" (W, I, 28).

Running through Emerson's philosophy is the basic relativity which language captures through its analogues and metaphors; for man is an analogist, and studies relations in all objects" (W, I, 27). Language originated in poetry; spiritual and moral values were originally expressed by natural symbols. "Parts of speech are metaphors, because the whole of nature is a metaphor of the human mind" (W, I, 32).

For this reason, the philosopher should put his confidence in the everyday, ordinary use of language. Emerson, at this point, sounds very much like the later Wittgenstein of the Investigations. There is an "irresistible rectitude of language," he tells his Harvard audience, so that it is "very little affected by local and temporary opinions, but always returning to the true line, and is thus the true philosopher." Resisting whim and private fancy corrects itself in the long run. Back of the transient uses of language are the "stable names in universal use," which points to the basic truths of nature and of mind. To these speculations twentieth-century philosophy has just arrived. Here we see, furthermore, the relativity of Emerson's view of language as well as its organic structure. Anticipating Walter B. Cannon's notion of homeostasis, he refers to the fixed average on which life depends and the stable truths of language, reflecting Nature and Mind; for his illustration he takes the thermometer which "has average points to which it often returns, so that the maker finds it necessary to fix these as determinate marks such as the freezing and the boiling point of water, the blood heat, and the zero, so language has, amid hourly and monthly variations, fixed averages which in years and ages are selfsame and secular."[29]

(B) Poetry. Emerson does not shrink from the serious poetical use of the modern scientific world-view. Singing of both Nature and Man as revelations of Divine Reason the poet does not deny his genius when he uses insight gained by the man of Nature (Science). The ultimate presupposition of Science (Reason) is seen by the poet to be the ultimate ground of all Being. The forms Science discloses as laws are the constant characteristics of organic beings, which give the basis for the unity of both the Arts and Science. The purpose of poetry, as Emerson expressed it in the essay on Poetry and Imagination, is "the perpetual endeavor to express the spirit of the thing; to pass the brute body, and search the life and reason which cause it to exist" (W, VIII, 17)--also the Mission of Science. But the discovery of the poet is that the value men set on substance has "a higher value as symbols; that nature is the universal shadow of man" (W, VIII, 23).

That group of poems called "Elements and Mottoes" best illustrates Emerson's incorporation of the principles of natural science into his poetry, for science is interpreted as the poetic revelation of mind. The mission of the poetic seems to be a heightened insight into the evolutionary processes of Nature (W, IX, 281):

A subtle chain of countless rings
The next unto the farthest brings;
The eye reads omens where it goes,
And speaks all languages the rose;
And, striving to be man, the worm
Mounts through all the spheres of form.

In Compensation (W, IX, 270), what had always been a continual concern of Emerson's is set on the background of the tenuous balance of natural forces:

The Wings of Time are black and white,
Pied with morning and with night.
Mountain tall and ocean deep
Trembling balance duly keep.
In changing moon and tidal wave
Glows the feud of Want and Have.

Again under Prudence (W, IX, 280), the practical development of technology out of science is poetically expressed:

Theme no poet gladly sung,
Fair to old and foul to young;
Scorn not thou the love of parts,
And the articles of arts.
Grandeur of the perfect sphere
Thanks the atoms that cohere.

Emerson's poetic view of Nature keeps pace with his interest in Natural History. His unique prose style becomes more intelligible from the same standpoint. "I am not anatomist. I see and wonder." He rejected analysis, but the classification and generalization of Natural History is constantly presupposed. But he also rejects introspection. He is observer and reporter. "I believe that the best is the Natural Method. Namely, by use in the normal way, not by introversion."[30] No brooding ego-centric thinker he. Mind at work, and Nature as its reflection, are what interest him.

(C) "The Secret Logic." Philosophers would do well to take seriously Dewey's comment on those who criticize Emerson for lack of method, continuity and logic, and as only a writer of maxims or proverbs. "The critic, to my mind," he writes, "but writes down his own incapacity to follow a logic that is finely wrought."[31] Emerson's logic is the logic of Classification. By arranging data according to their resemblances and differences, keeping in mind continually their natural setting and relations, Emerson follows the logic of nature. The general biological classifications, i.e., the phylum, class, order, family, on down to genus and species, looked at from one angle, are a series of proliferating classes, best likened to the growing tree, its trunk a phylum rooted in a kingdom (plant, animal, etc.) with branchings into the other classifications. Movement in this direction divides individuals according to ever-increasingly distinct Ideas. But movement in the other direction unifies according to ever-widening Ideas, until the whole phylum is organized, then all phyla under a kingdom and the three kingdoms (plant, animal, mineral) under the integrating Idea of Nature itself.

Emerson's thought moves in either direction according to what his purpose of classifying may be. But the latter is the basic justification for all other classification. Some Ideas are lost otherwise. Beauty, for instance, --"composite collective beauty which refuses to be analyzed. Nothing is beautiful alone. Nothing but is beautiful in the whole. Mark the day when the pine cones and acorns fall" (J, V, 26). Perhaps the best definition of the method of Natural History is given in the first lecture of his career: "It makes the intellect exact, quick to discriminate between the similar and the same, and greedy of truth" (EL, I, 18-19).[32] The year Nature appeared he summarized his logic in three points: "Here are two or three facts respecting Science. 1. The tendency to order and classification in the mind. 2. The correspondent Order actually subsisting in Nature. 3. Hence the humanity of science or the naturalness of knowing; the perception that the world was made by mind like ours; the recognition of design like ours; the seeing in the brutes analogous intelligence to ours" (J, V, 212).

IV.

There is something appealing about Emerson for each generation as there is in all the great philosophers. We note just two points of relevance to the philosophy of our times. First, his method of philosophizing and the results he gets from it put him among the process philosophers: Bergson, Whitehead, Hartshorne, and Teilhard de Chardin, each of whom applies philosophically the insights of modern natural sciences to the Phenomenon of Man. Second, Emerson's insights about the "transcendency of physics" and the "identity" of natural and moral laws, that "the axioms of physics translate the laws of ethics" and the "laws of moral nature answer to those of matter as face to face" (W, I, 32-33), are relevant in bridging the widening gap between the scientific and literary communities, or what C. P. Snow calls The Two Cultures (N.Y., 1963, p. 22). The scientist must face the question, "What is the meaning of my inquiry for the lives of myself and my fellowman?" Twentieth-century man, with an eye only to what he makes, fails to understand his technology and his science as a revelation of the power of Nature. Emerson, our most representative man, can help us find a meaningful unity once again, so that Nature will not appear foreign and alienated from our human problems but will become the metaphor of moral and intellectual life. In his final lectures he told the young men at Harvard: "Now this light, this glory, like the corona which astronomers have found around the sun, is real, and is the contribution of the mind; it is its announcement of the truth that is in Nature, and which the heart and the savage do not see, but which advancing science is ever uncovering."[33]

Memphis State University

---

1 The Complete Works of Ralph Waldo Emerson (Centenary Edition), ed. E. W. Emerson (Boston, 1903-1904), X, 262. (Hereafter called W.) References are to this edition as reprinted by William H. Wise (N.Y., 1929).

2 The Journals and Miscellaneous Notebooks of Ralph Waldo Emerson, ed. William H. Gilman et al., IV, ed. Alfred R. Ferguson (Cambridge, Mass., 1964), p. 200. (Hereafter called J.) Critical symbols and abbreviations will be omitted unless important to the argument. See J, I, xlix, for meaning of angle brackets and other editorial symbols.

3 Houghton Memorial Library (Hereafter called Houghton.) bMS Am 1280.200 (3). Natural History of the Intellect. I. "Powers and Laws of Thought," [1848]. Edward W. Emerson apparently wrote on the

front page of the manuscript, "What I have marked along margin with red pencil is printed in Natural History of Intellect, Vol. XII, Riverside Ed. EWE." These lectures are often confused with the much later Harvard series. Cf. Bliss Perry, Emerson Today (Princeton, 1931), pp. 44-45. The unpublished manuscripts of the later lectures were used by permission of the Harvard College Library and the Ralph Waldo Emerson Memorial Association. I wish to thank Professor W. H. Bond, Librarian, and Miss Carolyn Jakeman of The Houghton Library for their kind assistance. This work was supported by a grant from Memphis State University Faculty Research Fund.
4 See James Elliot Cabot, A Memoir of Ralph Waldo Emerson (Boston, 1887), II, p. 753. William Charvat, Emerson's American Lecture Engagements: A Chronological List (N.Y., 1961), pp. 46-47.
5 The Early Lectures of Ralph Waldo Emerson, 1833-1836, ed. Stephen E. Whicher and Robert E. Spiller (Cambridge, Mass., 1959), I, 5-25. (Hereafter called EL, I.) Volume II, 1838, ed. Stephen E. Whicher, Robert E. Spiller, and Wallace E. Williams (Cambridge, Mass., 1964) (Hereafter called EL, II).
6 See Kenneth Walter Cameron, A Commentary on Emerson's Early Lectures (Hartford, 1961), p. 28.
7 Cameron, p. 44.
8 Sherman Paul, Emerson's Angle of Vision: Man and Nature in American Experience (Cambridge, 1952), pp. 40-47. 9 Paul, p. 28.
10 Selected Poetry and Prose of Coleridge, ed. Donald A. Stauffer (N.Y., 1951), pp. 481-597).
11 Coleridge, p. 499.
12 Rudolf Magnus, Goethe as a Scientist, trans. Heinz Norden (N.Y., 1949), pp. 55-58.
13 See the discussion of Emerson's anticipation of Darwin's theory in Edward W. Emerson's "Biographical Sketch" of his father (W, I, xxix-xxx). On Lamarck's influence on Emerson, see Harry Hayden Clark, "Emerson and Science," Philological Quarterly, X (July, 1931), 225-260.
14 See Moncure Daniel Conway, Emerson at Home and Abroad (Boston, 1882), pp. 120ff. Conway notes the similarity in views between Darwin and Emerson, as well as the relative dates of their works mentioned in the text. He also notes the influence of Emerson's Nature on Tyndall, p. 150.
15 Alfred North Whitehead, Process and Reality: An Essay in Cosmology (N.Y., 1929), pp. 7-8.
16 A. L. de Jussieu, Genera Plantarum, reprint (N.Y., 1964), pp. xix-xxiii.
17 Houghton, bMS Am 1280.212 (1), pp. 8-9. He bagan this series of sixteen lectures at Harvard on April 26, 1870, on the topic he spent his life elaborating, "The Natural History of the Intellect." The next year he agreed to give them again. Originally scheduling eighteen lectures, the series was cut short. See Ralph L. Rusk, The Life of Ralph Waldo Emerson (N.Y., 1949), pp. 442-446. 18 Houghton, pp. 11-12.
19 Houghton, p. 13. See similar statement in earlier Natural History of Intellect (W, XII, 11).
20 Teilhard de Chardin, The Phenomenon of Man (N.Y., 1961, p. 31.
21 The Letters of Ralph Waldo Emerson, ed. Ralph L. Rusk (N.Y., 1939), II, p. 156.
22 William T. Harris, "The Dialectic Unity in Emerson's Prose," Jour. Spec. Phil., XVIII (April, 1884), 195-196. 23 Houghton, pp. 29-30. 24 Houghton, bMS Am 1280.212 (13), p. 19.
25 Cabot, Memoir, II, p. 639. 26 Houghton, bMS Am 1280.212 (13), p. 22.
27 Houghton, bMS Am 1280.212 (1), p. 37. 28 Houghton, p. 2. 29 Houghton, pp. 4-5. 30 Houghton, p. 9.
31 John Dewey, "Ralph Waldo Emerson" in Emerson: a Collection of Critical Essays, ed. Milton R. Konvitz and Stephen E. Whicher (Englewood Cliffs, 1962), p. 24.
32 See Cameron, p. 42, for sources of this precept. 33 Houghton, bMS 1280.212 (17), p. 32.

FIRST PERSON SUPERLATIVE: THE SPEAKER IN EMERSON'S ESSAYS

Is Emerson relevant today? One might reply that he is. He anticipates, that is, to a degree that is almost uncanny, the arguments for what is called relevance by today's young American scholars: that the past is of value only as it pertains to the needs of the present; that the individual should listen only to what speaks to him; that the learning experience is more important than the thing learned. All these propositions follow directly from Emerson's central principle of self-reliance, one definition of which is: "Do your thing & I shall know you."[2]

There is nothing strange, then, about the current Emerson revival, both in scholarship and in the classroom. At a time when romantic individualism is coming back into fashion it is natural to look to its

first American prophet. And yet when we do, we encounter straightway the great paradox in Emerson's individualism, which tends to disappoint the contemporary nonconformist once he sees it. The doctrine of self-reliance does not mean quite what it says: at bottom it means God-reliance; and all Emerson's celebrations of "individualism" boil down to the vision of individuality consumed in godhead. "The soul's emphasis is always right" (W, II, 145), but "the individual is always mistaken" (W, III, 69). Indeed, the discrepancy between the nominal and the real meanings of "self-reliance" is so extreme as to make the term seem like a rhetorical trick.

It is more than this, of course. After all, the way to the Self is through the self. Transcendence comes through inwardness. Nor is the Oversoul just a refuge for the timid introvert; it is natural for any individualist to want to feel supported by a higher moral law. Self-reliance, in short, lies somewhere in

between the extremes of willful subjectiveness and passive pietism, with a drift to the right as Emerson grew older. Nevertheless, having once "exposed" the latter side of Emerson, we might easily rest in the discovery, as one would not in the case of Thoreau, who, if anything, was more of a mystic than Emerson, though seemingly the greater individualist. Emerson's books are about general ideas; in most of the essays the infinite gets the last word, the external world having been left far behind. In Thoreau such cosmic excursions are brief; his books are set in nature and organized around specific personal experiences. Partly for this reason, Thoreau projects a more distinct and colorful personality; whereas he insists on the first person singular, Emerson seems rather to be trying to efface himself. It is impossible to imagine Emerson writing the second paragraph of Walden.

Still, this contrast is somewhat unfair. In particular, more attention needs to be paid than heretofore to the personal element in Emerson's prose. By this I mean not autobiographical content, not the relation between his essays and the course of his life, but autobiographical style: primarily, the sense of a persona as opposed to a mere editorial voice; and, secondarily, the use of any sort of local color to make the context more familiar, such as a reference to his life or surroundings. Until we take note of what Emerson does with such devices, no account of his work as an expression of his life, not even Stephen Whicher's Freedom and Fate, is going to dispel the impression that the essays are impersonal and abstract. True, critics have shown that his mental habit was to perceive the infinite through its particular manifestations, that in both his theory and use of language he put considerable emphasis on imagery and metaphor as vehicles for conveying abstract thought. In these and other ways, his literary style is sufficiently idiosyncratic to give the stamp of uniqueness to all he wrote. But originality with language is not the same thing as individuality of character. However strongly one responds to Emerson the writer as a subtle intellect or original artist, it is quite another thing to regard his writings as personal essays. I suspect that we tend to question his individualism so much more quickly than Thoreau's partly because we assume that in respect to the persona Emerson is an abstraction and wished to be taken as such. He may give us idealized self-portraits, like the Scholar or the Poet, but not direct self-revelation; he may allude to personal experience, but only for the sake of illustration.[3]

Emerson himself encouraged this view. "That which is individual & remains individual in my experience is of no value," he wrote in 1838. "What is fit to engage me & so engage others permanently, is what has put off its weeds of time & place & personal relation" (JMN, VII, 65). His literary criticism repeats the same maxims. The subjectiveness which is characteristic of the age, he writes in "Thoughts on Modern Literature," is a hopeful sign, as it marks "the uprise of the soul;" but we should be careful to distinguish between true and false subjectivity. A writer's use of the "I" is to be accepted or censured according as his work "leads us to Nature, or to the person of the writer. The great always introduce us to facts; small men introduce us always to themselves. The great man, even whilst he relates a private fact personal to him, is really leading us away from him to an universal experience" (W, XII, 313, 314-315). Here, as in all such pronouncements, Emerson deprecates subjective experience as such in favor of the universal truth it contains. His readers, from Edward Emerson on down, have said the same of his writing: that autobiographical "incidents are generalized and personality merged in a type" (W, XII, 470-471n). Emerson's reputation for personal reticence makes this assessment all the more plausible. Starting with some of his friends, Emerson watchers have always been quick to draw a parallel between his aloofness and the abstract level of his essays.

But is the traditional interpretation really faithful to the facts? Perhaps the best way to begin the inquiry is to consider Emerson's method of transposing thoughts and experiences from life to diary to lecture to essay. Among the thousands of instances, the majority seem to follow his stated purpose of winnowing away the circumstantial from the universal, to the point that one often cannot tell without the aid of the Journals that the passage derives from an actual experience. Take for example this sentence from Nature: "In the tranquil landscape, and especially in the distant line of the horizon, man beholds somewhat as beautiful as his own nature (W, I, 10). This could be a purely cerebral improvisation, especially the figure of the horizon as symbolic of the circumference of the soul. As it happens, the sentence has a more personal basis. "I went to Walden Pond this evening a little before sunset, and in the tranquil landscape I behold somewhat as beautiful as my own nature" (JMN, V, 189). But in revising, Emerson eliminates local detail, adds intellectual complexity (there is no sign of the horizon metaphor in the journal version), and turns a particular experience into a general proposition. Actually, the result is even more abstract than it needs to be--the rest of the paragraph in Nature is first person. Altogether

it would seem as if, in transposing, Emerson's mind was not on the experience itself but on the subtle formulation into which he was able to convert it. And so the passage gains in literary charm but at the cost of some immediacy.

But if we look at the rest of the paragraph to which the above sentence serves as the conclusion, we get a very different impression. Its high points are two instances of inspiration through nature, both reported by a persona: the metamorphosis into transparent eyeball and the sensation of joy upon crossing the common. The second experience is more generalized, taking place merely "in the woods," anytime, anywhere; Emerson tries to recreate the sense of the infinite primarily through rhetorical flourish. The first is localized--on "a bare common, in snow puddles, at twilight, under a clouded sky"--and relies more upon the imagery for its impact. Both passages happen to be re-workings of actual experiences reported in the journal; and, most interesting, in the journal versions there is no appreciable difference between the two, in rhetorical level. For purposes of publication, Emerson inflated the second and made the first more homely. Passage two originated with a feeling "as I walked in the woods" on March 19, 1835 (JMN, V, 18); in revising, he softened the sense of specificity and added such ornamentation as the symbolic eyeball, which is not in the journal. But the original version of the other passage begins simply "I rejoice in Time. I do not cross the common without a wild poetic delight notwithstanding the prose of my demeanour" (JMN, IV, 355). This is *less* personal, *less* anecdotal than the corresponding sentence in *Nature*. Contrary to what one might expect from Emerson's strictures about the use of the subjective in art, he revised this passage so as to increase the illusion of specificity. Indeed, the whole chapter seems designed to do the same thing. As Richard Francis observes, it functions in the structure of *Nature* as a counterweight to Emerson's preliminary definitions, as "a highly personal statement about how we perceive what has just been defined."[4] The message it seems to convey is: Reader, whatever we conclude from the formal analysis of nature that will follow, the original relation to the universe exists, for I have experienced it. Perhaps the chapter is called "Nature" for this reason: because the experiences there described epitomize the philosophy of the whole book.

Emerson does not make this point overbearingly. On the contrary, he takes some pains to make his speaker represent the reader's experiences too. For instance, the chapter begins: "To go into solitude, a man needs to retire as much from his chamber as from society. I am not solitary whilst I read and write, though nobody is with me. But if a man would be alone, let him look at the stars" (W, I, 7). By alternating here between "I" and "a man" and by making "I" the subject of a proposition we can easily accept, Emerson persuades us that his first person is universal. The "I" could easily be changed to "one." In this sense, Emerson is quite within the limits of his theory of subjectivity. But the part that the theory leaves out, or underplays, is that the first person adds a special tone to the context--not autobiography, exactly, but still the sense of personal witness. The fact that the "I" represents himself here as a solitary writer adds to the impression that the author is speaking in his own person. And when we catch Emerson occasionally transposing from journal to essay circumstantial facts which are completely extrinsic to his message--"The charming landscape which I saw *this morning*" (W, I, 8); "Not less excellent...was the charm, *last evening*, of a January sunset" (W, I, 17); etc. [italics mine] it becomes clear that he must have consciously striven for such coloring. This impression is further strengthened as one notes, now and then, additional cases where an essay passage is made more personal than its original. For instance, the "reminiscences" of the devil's child in "Self-Reliance" (W, II, 50), the orthodox preacher in "Compensation" (W, II, 94-95), and the "certain poet" in "The Poet" (W, III, 22) all seem to be fabrications.[5]

The chapter just analyzed, then, is not an isolated example. The personal element recurs throughout Emerson's prose, on the average of about eight to ten passages per essay, but sometimes much more often. In addition to *Nature*, perhaps the most significant instances are "Self-Reliance," "Friendship," "Experience," "New England Reformers," "Montaigne," "Worship," "Illusions," *English Traits*, and Emerson's contribution to the *Memoirs of Margaret Fuller Ossoli*. In all these works, the personal element is exploited far more than Emerson's reputation for impersonality would lead us to expect.

This personal element, however, is not so much an entity as a composite of two rather different first-person forms, each of which has its own effect, though they appear side by side. We have seen them both in action; now let us define them a bit more closely. One is the voice of private feeling or opinion, as in "What right have I to write on Prudence, whereof I have little" (W, II, 221); "I confess to an extreme tenderness of nature on this point" (W, II, 195); "I do not find the religions of men at this moment

very creditable to them" (W, VI, 207); and "I prefer a tendency to stateliness to an excess of fellowship" (W, III, 136). The speaker in all these sentences is aware of himself as separate from his audience, aware of possible disagreements or misunderstandings, which make it necessary for him to confess or pontificate.

This self-consciousness is not true of the other voice. It is exemplary or representative; it asks you to take what is said not just as opinion but as axiom: e.g., "I am not solitary whilst I read and write;" "I am made immortal by apprehending my possession of incorruptible goods" (W, IV, 22); or "I am always environed by myself" (W, III, 98). This is the "I" which in its more ambitious moments we think of as "transcendental," as in "I can even with a mountainous aspiring say, I am God" (JMN, V, 336). Its pervasiveness in Emerson's writing, that is, has a partly philosophical basis, in the idea that the individual can speak for the universal. Emerson himself clarifies the strategy in a rare bit of self-exegesis: "A great man is coming to eat at my house. I do not wish to please him; I wish that he should wish to please me. I will stand here for humanity, and though I would make it kind, I would make it true" (W, II, 60; italics mine). As in the journal passage just quoted, here we have the two voices side by side, the private voice explaining what the exemplary voice proclaims. The latter is the Emersonian counterpart to Whitman's speaker in "Song of Myself" and Jones Very's poetic impersonations of God and Christ. In each case, the author's defense against the charge of egoism, or blasphemy, is that he is speaking according to the informing spirit, rather than as an individual.

Doubtless it was this second persona for which Emerson was really contending, in "Thoughts on Modern Literature" and elsewhere, as the proper use of the subjective. And his preference for what was universal in a man's work, as against what was merely personal, increased, too, as he grew older. In Nature the poet is pictured as a hero who subdues the world to the service of his imagination (W, I, 51-54); in "The Poet" he is reduced to a mere medium for recording the poetry which "was all written before time was" (W, III, 8).[6] Upon turning from Emerson's criticism to his style, however, one finds a precisely opposite trend. The voice of private opinion is used more and more; the essays become more anecdotal; the speaker seems increasingly ready to speak off the top of his head; one sees more and more fillers like "Here is a lesson which I brought along with me in boyhood from the Latin School" (W, VI, 195).

Perhaps Representative Men marks the beginning of this trend, to the extent that it could be subtitled "my favorite people"--though Emerson is still a long way from the tone of the cozy, crochety old scholar that one finds in "Books." One step closer is his memoir of Margaret Fuller. Here he goes into a surprising amount of detail about how Margaret affected him--how she impressed him upon first acquaintance, the ups and downs of their friendship, and so forth. Finally, in English Traits, the man Emerson emerges for the first time as the central character in his own writing. The main subject is, of course, the people and things he saw, but we also learn in detail how he fared on his voyage (W, V, 25-33), how he got one-up on his English friends (287-288), and how "I made the acquaintance of De Quincey, of Lord Jeffrey," and a host of other names (294). Altogether English Traits contains much less personal trivia than most travel books, but for Emerson it is positively gossipy. The essays are never quite the same again. His later works mark a return to the general-idea-essay format, but with a shade of difference which is well-illustrated by the following passages on the same general theme, from "Manners" and "Behavior," respectively.

> ...I dislike a low sympathy of each with his neighbor's needs. Must we have a good understanding with one another's palates? as foolish people who have lived long together know when each wants salt or sugar. I pray my companion, if he wishes for bread, to ask me for bread, and if he wishes for sassafras or arsenic, to ask me for them, and not to hold out his plate as if I knew already (W, III, 137-138).

> Every hour will show a duty as paramount as that of my whim just now, and yet I will write it,--that there is one topic peremptorily forbidden to all well-bred, to all rational mortals, namely, their distempers. If you have not slept, or if you have slept, or if you have headache, or sciatica, or leprosy, or thunderstroke, I beseech you by all angels to hold your peace, and not pollute the morning, to which all the housemates bring serene and pleasant thoughts, by corruption and groans (W, VI, 196).

In both passages the private voice is speaking; and the burden is much the same: The speaker is requesting

us, with some impatience and sarcasm, to maintain a little decorum. But the second tirade exposes the speaker more. The persona in "Manners" knows where he is going; he is confident of his authority over the reader; his language is crisp and peremptory. The other man is a bit fuddled. He is not sure, in the first sentence, whether his thought is worth saying. In the second, he becomes long-winded--the comic hyperbole takes much longer to unwind than in the last sentence of the first excerpt--so that the "beseeching" suggests impotence, where the "I pray" in the other passage sounds like a command. Altogether, the Emerson of "Behavior" seems a tiny bit like a garrulous, scolding grandfather, who runs on even as he is aware that he may be ignored. Thus the posture is more revealing: in "Manners" we are being given orders by someone whom we don't quite know; in "Behavior" the speaker says more about himself, probably, than he intended.

Of equal importance with this development is what happens to the exemplary persona during the course of Emerson's career. It is used often and to great effect through Essays II, but after that it largely dwindles away. "In my daily work I incline to repeat my old steps.... But some Petrarch or Ariosto, filled with the new wine of his imagination...smiles and arouses me with his shrill tones, breaks up my whole chain of habits, and I open my eye on my own possibilities" (W, II, 312-313). So Emerson writes in "Circles." In "Illusions" a similar thought becomes: "I, who have all my life heard any number of orations and debates, read poems and miscellaneous books, conversed with many geniuses, am still the victim of any new page" (W, VI, 316). The intent of both passages is precisely the same--to illustrate the power of the poet. But in the second, the "I" is given a biography, so that the statement comes out less like testimonial than soliloquy. Equally common is for the exemplary persona to give way to an impersonal construction. "I can see my own vices without heat in the distant persons of Solomon, Alcibiades, and Catiline" (W, II, 5), Emerson says in "History." The sentence can be duplicated in Representative Men, but the emphasis of that work is on history rather than on the experiencer.

Neither of these two examples should be surprising. As to the first, it is logical that the exemplary persona should wane as the private one increases: there is an inverse relation between the particular and the cosmic. Self-consciousness and biographical detail are at odds with universality, once they become very prominent. Likewise, as to the second, the more conscious one is of himself as a limited, private person, the less likely he will be to identify with Alcibiades. Both of these shifts, furthermore, are consistent with what we know about the development of Emerson's thought as a whole. It became progressively harder for him to affirm the soul's ability to master the Not-me, as he had done in Nature. He dwelt more on human limits. And so, in his rhetoric, understandably, it became harder for him to represent his persona as universal, and more normal for him to take the position of observer. It would seem, then, that the basis of Emerson's repudiation of false subjectivity in his criticism, namely his sense of individual fallibility, was the very thing which led him increasingly into it in his later writing. For example, "Experience" has a more confessional air than "Self-Reliance," even as it takes a lower estimate of man, because the speaker admits a greater disparity between self and Self than he had supposed.

Ought we then to prefer the later Emerson, as being more personal, more familiar? After all, if it was a weakness in him to sink himself in his generalizations, one might suppose that his later writing would have more appeal. But such is by no means the case. Today, especially, most readers--myself included--seem to find early Emerson far more vigorous, fresh, and exciting, and later Emerson comparatively tame and vapid. The factors which account for this reaction range far beyond the one I am considering, but the use of the personal element does, I think, enter in. First, the exemplary persona, despite its generalized character, has a personality of its own, and a far more appealing one than the dominant voice of the later essays. I have sketched it in part already. It believes in its own universality; it has a tremendous imaginative reach, as in "I am God in nature; I am a weed by the wall" (W, II, 307), or "I am always insincere, as always knowing there are other moods" (W, III, 247). In short, it is an extremely uncompromising character. When it appears it often gives the sense of great emotional stake and commitment, as in this passage from "Friendship:" "I ought to be equal to every relation. It makes no difference how many friends I have and what content I can find in conversing with each, if there be one to whom I am not equal. If I have shrunk unequal from one contest, the joy I find in all the rest becomes mean and cowardly" (W, II, 200). This would sound impressive even if Emerson took it all back in the next paragraph (as partly he does). In substance, the passage is only half of a rather nebulous equivocation about what to expect from friendship, but the mode of statement here gives it the force of a personal credo.

Secondly, the private voice, in early Emerson, reinforces this tone and gives it more concreteness. As we saw in comparing "Manners" and "Behavior," the private voice changes not just in frequency but in character too. Several times in the early essays, for instance, it appears in the form of what might be called "disclaimers"--points when Emerson steps unexpectedly outside his train of thought and makes, momentarily, as if to throw it all aside. As in Nature: "But I own there is something ungrateful in expanding too curiously the particulars of...idealism. I have no hostility to nature, but a child's love to it" (W, I, 59). Or in "History:" "Is there somewhat overweening in this claim? Then I reject all I have written..." (W, II, 39). Or--best known--in "Circles:" "Let me remind the reader that I am only an experimenter... an endless seeker with no Past at my back" (W, II, 318). I find no such audacity in the later essays. But it is quite characteristic of the exemplary voice and adds to the impression of a flesh-and-blood author who is prepared to back up in his actions his most intransigent words about self-reliance.

Thinking of passages like the one last quoted, Jonathan Bishop calls the Emersonian speaker an "experimental self."[7] That seems to me an admirable way of summing up the foregoing analysis of the subject, providing we recognize an ambivalence in the word "experimental." The characteristic speaker in the early essays is experimental chiefly in its nineteenth-century usage as a religious term, meaning "experiential," having to do with religious experience. For in the early essays, the speaker is primarily an experiencer of the holy, ready to take on the protean manifestations of the soul in nature--to make himself equal to every relation--and to deny them all, too, if the spirit demands. The later speaker, by contrast, is eminently an observer, experimental in the sense of testing out all possibilities but embracing none. The distinction, of course, is not hard and fast--nothing is in Emerson--but it is clear enough, as in the attitude of the speaker in the first chapter of Nature, versus his attitude in the introduction to "Illusions," a slightly long-winded account of an expedition to Mammoth Cave. In the first, nature is felt as possibility; in the second, possibility is frustration. Each stance has its own appeal, but the first is truer to the original notion of self-reliance, which stresses the potential authoritativeness of intuition as opposed to its potential inaccuracy.

In conclusion, then, Emerson's attitude toward subjectivity in writing was fundamentally sound, according to his own doctrine. The Emersonian speaker is most himself when his pronouncements come across also as universal laws. But Emerson might have emphasized, too, that these laws depend, for full effect, upon the sense of an experiencer. "Though I prize my friends, I cannot afford to talk with them and study their visions, lest I lose my own" (W, II, 215). How much more telling this is in the first person than in the third, or even the second! Emerson must have known as much, or he would not have used a persona so often, or retained so much circumstantial detail, or fabricated an occasional anecdote. Why then did his criticism short-shrift these devices? Probably for the same reason that he disparaged "talent" as opposed to "genius" despite his own attention to craftsmanship and his dislike of its neglect in others: he took the matter for granted. In Emerson's method of composition, the private experience was a given; it was where he started; the universal dimension was what he sought to attain. Just as he saw the danger of structural eccentricity from composing by collation of journal snippets, he saw that to base his essays on his daily experience might betray him into egoism. And on both counts he grew more sensitive as he aged, because on both counts his fears were borne out. The later essays shows less synthesizing power and more and more of the self with a small "s." Somewhat the same thing happened to Thoreau.

Indeed, the difference between the two writers in respect to the persona, as in most others, is one of degree and not kind. Emerson's most characteristic speaker is representative but also humanized somewhat; Thoreau's is more closely drawn but also plays stylized archetypal roles--such as the quester and the hermit--were it not for which, Thoreau would have had far less of an impact on his readers than has been the case.[7] Altogether, the two writers deserve to be grouped together with the many other romanticist writers of the last two centuries who use a double persona, and especially with their transcendental kindred, notably Whitman and Very--for the motif is intensified in transcendentalist writing, because of its preoccupation with the subject of the individual's nearness to godhead. Whether we prefer Emerson's version of the double persona, or Thoreau's, or Whitman's, or Very's, is a matter of taste. If we reject Emerson's, he certainly will not complain; he would have been the first to recoil at the idea of his books' being forced on anyone as required reading. But any such rejection should be an informed one. Emerson should not be dismissed as a transparent eyeball, though it is amusing to poke fun at that side of him. His affirmation of the first person superlative begins in his art, as it did in his life, with the sense of the first person particular.

Oberlin College

1 I should like to express my gratitude to the Howard Foundation for assisting my research on Emerson with a generous fellowship, without which this paper could not have been completed.
2 The Journals and Miscellaneous Notebooks of Ralph Waldo Emerson, ed. William Gilman, et al. (Cambridge, 1960-), VII, 225. Hereafter cited as JMN. All quotations from Emerson's essays are from the Centenary Edition of his works, which is cited as W.
3 Actually, very little has been written about any aspect of the Emersonian persona. The only sustained discussion of the speaker in the essays, so far as I know, in Jonathan Bishop's provocative chapter on "Tone" in Emerson on the Soul (Cambridge, 1964), though even it is devoted to exploring Emerson's tonal richness and variety rather than the device of the speaker itself. Another part of Bishop's study which has stimulated my essay, again in a different direction, is his reading of the first chapter of Nature, (pp. 10-15).
4 "The Architectonics of Emerson's Nature," reprinted in Merton M. Sealts, Jr. and Alfred R. Ferguson, eds., Emerson's "Nature:" Origin, Growth, Meaning (N.Y. and Toronto, 1969), p. 168. I am also indebted to this book for its index of journal and lecture passages used in Nature.
5 For the first two examples, cf. JMN, V, 48-49; and JMN, VII, 182-183, respectively. That the encounter reported in "The Poet" is a fabrication is clear from the previous draft of the passage in "Genius," the fifth lecture in the unpublished "Human Life" series, pp. 12-12v. (MS. in Houghton Library, Harvard.)
6 This is not to imply that the difference between the two positions is absolute. But there is a marked shift of emphasis. Cf. on this point Stephen Whicher, Freedom and Fate: An Inner Life of Ralph Waldo Emerson (Philadelphia, 1961), pp. 136-140.
7 Op. cit., p. 130.
8 Two illuminating discussions of Thoreau's persona as archetype are Joseph J. Moldenhauer, "Paradox in Walden," The Graduate Journal, VI (1964), 132-146; and Charles R. Anderson, The Magic Circle of Walden (N.Y., Chicago, and San Francisco, 1968), pp. 47-56.

THE CRISIS OF ALIENATION IN EMERSON'S EARLY THOUGHT

LEWIS P. SIMPSON

This is the amount of all our insight into nature, the discovery of the purpose; and wherever we are at fault in our search our whole views become loose & unsettled; the fact where the study fails is regarded as monstrous.--Emerson, Journals (1823)

Emerson published Nature in his thirty-third year. Until this event in the fall of 1836, he had offered no unusual promise to the world. When he had graduated from Harvard fifteen years before, he had won a place no higher than the dead center of mere competence. He was number thirty in a class of fifty-nine; and if his deportment had not been exemplary, he probably would have been lower in the standings. Following this undistinguished entry into the world, he had, quite reluctantly, done a little school teaching. Subsequently he had attended the Harvard Divinity School, had been licensed to preach, and eventually had been ordained. Accepting a call to the Second Church in Boston, he had within less than four years announced that he could no longer celebrate the Lord's Supper and had resigned his pastorate. This had caused a small stir, but he had soon left the scene for an extended European journey. Then in 1836 he issued a dramatic manifesto asserting the radical freedom of the modern mind. A man well past thirty who had never seemed to be more than a mild and somewhat uncertain rebel, Emerson appears to have had a more or less sudden illumination or revelation.

In a way that happened. But careful students of Emerson are coming to understand that the apparent uncertainty and tentativeness of his early career are quite deceptive. During this period his "Foundation and Ground-Plan," as Carlyle called Nature, was thoroughly meditated. Indeed in his youthful years Emerson experienced an interesting and critical episode in what he once called "the interior and spiritual history of New England:" its coming into the modern philosophical and poetic sensibility. Nature does not record, properly speaking, a beginning. It marks the climax and the resolution of a long crisis in the mind of a precocious seeker struggling to discover and to come to grips with, one of the central modern problems--the relationship between knowledge as an institution and knowledge as consciousness. Or, it may be said, between knowledge as doubt and knowledge as wonder--in some ultimate sense between knowledge as Appearance and knowledge as Being. If this is the case--and I would urge that it is--I can scarcely attempt

to describe Emerson's early thought in a short essay. Perhaps, however, I can suggest the importance of recognizing the broad configurations of the story, emotional and intellectual, of Emerson's thought in the 1820's. I shall be especially concerned with the mid 1820's, when Emerson was settled on preparing for a ministerial career and scarcely conceived of any other way of life.

I

As it comes to us in his Journals and letters, the story of Emerson's mind before the publication of Nature is a drama (and the dramatic quality must be emphasized) interwoven with and intimately related to, poverty, illness, and death. When the Reverend William Emerson died in 1812, his family was left in a state of not very genteel poverty. Glimpses of the consequences of this deprivation are afforded in Ralph L. Rusk's highly detailed biography of Emerson: the necessary sale at auction of the father's small but treasured library; Ralph as a little boy seeking desperately among fallen poplar leaves for a lost dollar bill he had been given to buy shoes with; Ralph and his brother Edward forced to share a single coat and to face the taunt of their schoolmates, "Whose turn is it to wear the coat today?" and the Emerson boys' heroically giving their last loaf of bread to one even poorer than they. Later on poverty forced Emerson to tax his precarious health and to delay his preparation for the ministry by becoming a "hopeless," "droning" schoolmaster in his brother William's finishing school for young Boston ladies. "Hope, it is true, still hangs out, though at a further remove, her gay banners," he confided to his Journals at this period of his life; "but I have found her a cheat once, twice, many times, and shall I trust the deceiver again?" Bad health and recurrent, serious sickness hampered him more than lack of money. Tuberculosis ("the mouse in my chest," he called it) was a family curse that threatened his life for years. In addition, he suffered severely from other ailments, particularly rheumatic pains and occasionally from decided impairment of vision. Often seriously ill, he was at other times "not sick, not well," just irritatingly "luke-sick." In either case, as with poverty, "the worst part of sickness was the deferring of hopes," which made him "heart sick." His spells of "heart sickness" bordered on what today might be diagnosed as spells of psychic depression, when he had agonizing doubts about his personality. Neither poverty nor illness was as hard on young Emerson as several intense bereavements: the death of Ellen Tucker Emerson, his first wife, and of two beloved brothers, Edward and Charles. Within eighteen months after his marriage to Ellen in 1827--during which Emerson says his bride was "playful & social" even when "her sociability" was "imprisoned in whispers"--she was dead of the common scourge, tuberculosis. Emerson was never to be released from the presence of the "one person in the world in whose separate existence as a soul" he "could so readily and fully believe." The early deaths of Edward and Charles were scarcely less difficult for him. Edward died of tuberculosis in Puerto Rico in 1834, concluding, Emerson said, "the short life of a silent poet & silent orator." Two years later the same disease destroyed Charles, on the verge of what might well have been a distinguished career in law and politics. In terrible loneliness, Emerson asked, "When one has never had but little society--and all that society is taken away--what is there worth living for?" At the moment it seemed to him that if poverty and illness had chastened him, death had confounded him.

Yet out of unpropitious beginnings, and from low states of spirit close at times to despair, he came forth to proclaim in Nature a vision of the autonomy and power of the individual consciousness that can only be compared to celebrations of the creative force of the individual will in Blake, Kierkegaard, Nietzche, and in his own disciple, Thoreau. How did he overcome the critical deprivations of his childhood and early manhood? Part of the answer at least lies in their relation to the ethic of ambition he subscribed to. Emerson was born into the discipline of what Oliver Wendell Holmes termed the "Academic Races" of New England, a class of men of letters drawn heavily from ministerial families but representing the professions of teaching and law as well as the ministry--who assumed responsibility for the moral and intellectual and literary condition of their culture. Bred for this responsibility, or in some cases recruited for it by its blood-and-bone hereditary members, the New England men of letters in the nineteenth century made up a group approximating Coleridge's notion of a "clerisy." Guided by an amalgam of classical and Christian virtues--the compound of values young Emerson called "Virtue"--the members of the New England clerisy were given to translating the ills of life from deprivations into positive resources of the spirit. Virtue demanded that one triumph over unfortunate circumstances. Virtue's commandment was what Emerson felt when, in his mature years, he refused to waste sympathy on a poor boy, as poor as he himself had once been, who hesitated to go to college. "Go to Cambridge & eat bread & water & live to think," Emerson told him. Virtue sustained Emerson when, alone in faraway Florida on what seemed to be an almost desperate mission to restore his sick lungs, he wrote to his Aunt Mary: "He has seen but half the Universe who

never has been shown the house of Pain. Pleasure and peace are but indifferent teachers of what it is life to know."[1]

We find, however, that young Emerson did not altogether accept the official ethic of ambition in his world. His knowledge of pain and death qualified as well as stimulated his eagerness for success. A reflection from his Journals in March, 1824, is of interest: "Shall I embroil my short life with a vain desire of perpetuating its memory when I am dead & gone in this dirty planet? I complain daily of my world, that it is false, disappointing, imperfect, & uncomfortable; & reason would that I should get thro' it as silently & hastily as I can & especially avoiding to tie any hopes or fears to it. I make it my boast that I am the citizen of a far country far removed from the low influences of earth & sea, of time & change; that my highly destined nature spurns its present abode & aspires after a mode of existence & a fellowship of beings which shall eclipse & efface the gaudy glory of this. When my body shall be in the clods my triumphant soul, glad of any deliverance, will think no more of it or its habitation. Am I then to give my days & nights to a gnawing solicitude to get me a reputation, a fame, forsooth among these worm-eaten, worm-eating creatures of clay, these boys of the universe, these infants of immortality as they all must be while they live on earth? Virtue says Go beg the impartial goddess to enrol your name on her historic scroll. Why? Because if you toil & deserve to write your name there, you will effectually contribute by the same efforts to the good of yourself & your species. The attempt is very laudable, even if it fail of success. The 'ambition of immortality is chimerical' to all but a few. But in many instances doubtless the silver trumpets of angels will answer to the flourishes to earthly fame. As in case of Newton, Socrates, Howard, & more--"[2]

Worldly fame, the instrument of virtue in perpetuating and extending knowledge for the good of the individual and the race, was a standard attitude in the humanistic value system of the Academic Races. But in his somber meditation, Emerson questioned as well as upheld the validity of the quest for fame. He was drawn to the Christian rejection of the world, conceiving himself to be a stranger and a pilgrim on "this dirty planet," fixing his vision on his citizenship in "a far country." Underlying this desire to reject the world unquestionably was something at times approaching physical and emotional exhaustion. Poverty, illness, and death--particularly at this point illness--taxed Emerson's capacity to respond to the ethic of the clerisy. But in entertaining the vision of a beatified citizenship in a far country, Emerson was failing to respond not simply to this ethic but also to an anxiety in Western civilization rising from intimations of doubt about the value of the institutional concept of knowledge. Forced by the deprivations of his life into the role of the introspective observer of his age, young Emerson experienced in an intimate and graphic way the modern breakdown of the assurance that the accumulation of knowledge is the true vocation of the mind. The best way to understand this situation is to approach Emerson's early thought not in the conventional way through his break with Unitarianism but through the wider drama his thought became when his estrangement from the "liberal religion" or the "rational religion" or the "Boston religion," as it was variously called, is considered in the light of the character of the literary mind of Boston. I mean especially its domination by one of the historic, controlling notions of Western civilization, the concept of "the progress of letters."

II

The emergence of this idea in the Boston-Cambridge world, which goes back to the founding of Harvard, reveals its relation to a complex of attitudes, which include the ancient concept of the transfer of letters and learning from pre-Athenian seats of learning to Athens, to Rome, to Paris, to London, to America (not least to Boston). John Adams spoke for the general educational experience of his community when he observed, "There is nothing in my little reading, more ancient in my memory than the observation that arts, sciences, and empire traveled westward; and in conversation it was always added since I was a child, that their next leap would be over the Atlantic into America."[3] Another attitude strongly present in the theme of the progress of letters is the preservation of society from the effects of the love of money and luxury. Perhaps the most important attitude, however, derives from its association with the eighteenth-century metaphysic of linear progress--the idea that human knowledge (knowledge as conceived before the age of specialization) is a perfectible institution--strikingly illustrated in a plea made in 1807 for the patronage of the newly established Boston Athenaeum, which was an enterprise of the Boston-Cambridge clerisy, including Emerson's father, the Reverend William Emerson, the first president of the Anthology Society and a dedicated man of letters: "Among the many literary and scientifick establishments, which

have been thought worthy of the patronage of influence and wealth, that of large repositories of books has justly been considered as most illustrious for its dignity, its importance, and its pleasures. The history of learned libraries is the history of power consecrated to learning. It celebrates the patronage of monarchs, the munificence of a splended nobility, the support of a lettered clergy, and the liberality of cultivated gentlemen. The generous aid of rank, opulence, and influence proceeds from the intrinsick excellence of the subject. Whatever is intellectual is a portion of the supreme reason, and proportionally as it is free from corruption, approaches nearer the fountain. The operations of this principle are recorded in volumes. The earliest of these is almost coeval with the primary institutions of society, and from that period to the present the mass of human knowledge, notwithstanding the diminutions it has suffered, and the obstructions it has encountered, has accumulated from age to age, and has descended from generation to generation, till its present possessors are captivated in admiring the variety of its parts, the beauty of its materials, or are lost in contemplating its extensive magnitude, its diversified splendour, and its irresistible power."[4]

This kind of excited devotion to the institutional power of letters and learning--embodied in the library, the university, the literary society--was an intimate part of Emerson's education. He was brought up in a community in which his father was but one of several highly energetic men of letters. Man like Joseph Stevens Buckminster, William Tudor, William Smith Shaw, Andrews Norton, and George Ticknor were not mere forerunners but shapers of the Boston-Cambridge literary world of the nineteenth century. Young Emerson accepted as germane to the literary life the crucial necessity his father's generation felt in their literary endeavors: the preservation of civilization against barbarism. Emerson accepted as axiomatic, as he puts it in "Wide World XIII," "the superiority of a civilized to a savage nation & of the educated to the uneducated part of a community." How "discouraging to the cause of Education" it would be, he pondered, "if Newtons, Bacons, & Lockes were as often bred in shops & stables as in colleges." Such, however, is not the case; for "the fact is that <u>all</u> genius has owed its development to literary establishments." Self-made Benjamin Franklin, Emerson recognized, had formed himself on the institutional character of knowledge. What if Franklin had been born a New Zealand native? It might be that he "would have been a clever swimmer, boatman & weather prophet...but he would certainly not have left an institution or a name."[5] He would not have left the American Philosophical Society and other institutions he established to represent the progress of letters in the new nation--institutions which had taken their places in the advancement of knowledge Emerson saw continuing, according to divine purpose, into the later age: "All objects in the universe, far as the eye can reach & thought can comprehend them, fulfill some purpose, and are parts of some plan; and whatsoever things the infancy of knowledge once regarded as exceptions to this prevailing order, the advancement of knowledge has brought in to fill a chasm in the regular series of things & beings. Mind, which in human nature creeps on its long journey [he first wrote "on its progress"] to the source of things with a snail's pace, (compared with the intellects he is fond of imagining,) by the excellent necessity of its nature, <u>expands</u>, as it proceeds; and, in this late age, when it looks no longer with the timid glance of a child, but with the experienced eye of Centuries into the bosom of nature, it is able to unite things severed by long intervals, to compare mean beginnings with remote & mighty results, & thus to restore order to a Chaos of mighty things, where, in time past the grandeur of the object outwent the capacity of the Observer; so that even the slow & halting march of human science continually discovers the divine adjustment to circumstances to fulfill purposes."[6]

Yet in his youthful years when he was inescapably drawn toward the unqualified acceptance of the progress of letters, both as a metaphysic and a value system, he was asking deep questions about the validity of the concept. This questioning, implied and overt in his writings in the 1820's, grew out of and was an extension of his questioning of the adequacy of Unitarianism, but only partly. With his propensity always to enter upon wide speculation, he was an inquirer into universal problems as much as or more than he was into particular Unitarian doctrines. This tendency is apparent in the passage from his <u>Journals</u> just given; and more so in what immediately follows in the same entry: "This is the amount of all our insight into nature, the discovery of purpose; and wherever we are at fault in our search our whole views become loose & unsettled; the fact where the study fails is regarded as monstrous. Now, in all the varieties of this investigation the question recurs to the investigator--What is the purpose of Man? Or is all nature, from sun & stars, to the root & the clod--instinct & dignified with design, & Man alone, the thinking inhabitant & the peerless lord of all--an insulated & casual creation? In this vast theatre of being, in the tremendous uncertainty that shuts up the future around the present activity of Nature's immense family of worlds & beings; what, where I pray you, is his security from its possible convulsions? Is his lot cast

upon the waters of chance? Is he unallied to Nature & independent of God? Then when Change & Destruction, those terrible agents in the Universe, obey their lord, & take hold on life & matter & dissipate the parent elements, when Thought is gathered through all its infinite channels to its Divine Fountain, & Goodness to its reward, & Matter is dissolved--then can his will bridle the ministers of the Universe, & stop their almighty operation? But the man who thus denies a moral design to his existence, thus sets himself adrift upon wild and unknown seas."[7]

We think of Pascal "swallowed up in the infinite immensities of space," feeling himself "terrified" and "astonished" at his condition. To believe in the "moral design" of the "vast theatre of being" so conceived requires more than a rational faith in the advancement of knowledge. I think we may refer to two letters, broadly speculative in import, that Emerson wrote to his Aunt Mary in the 1820's for the more overt beginnings of his rebellion against the institutional sensibility of knowledge. Their importance is increased by the fact that they were written to a person of remarkable intellect and "faithful lover" of the "mysteries of Providence," who was a doubter who, as Emerson realized later, refused to admit to doubt. She was, significantly, the only confidant Emerson had in his younger days who was his intellectual peer. What, he asked Aunt Mary in one letter written in 1823, is the purpose served in making the mysteries of Providence inexplicable? "Does the Universe great & glorious in its operation aim at the slight of a mountebank who produces a wonder among the ignorant by concealing the causes of unexpected effects?" He then pushed on through a series of momentous questions, centering on the problem of why a benevolent God allows evil and punishes it by death. He worked up to the "Gordian knot" of freedom of the will, and then revealed a strong influence that had worked on him even in his undergraduate days, the writings of David Hume. "Who is he that can stand up before him [Hume] & prove the existence of the Universe, & of its Founder? He hath an adroiter wit than all his forefathers in philosophy if he will confound this Uncircumcised. The long & dull procession of Reasoners that have followed since, have challenged the awful shade to duel, & struck the air with their puissant arguments. But as each new comer blazons 'Mr. Hume's objections' on his pages, it is plain they are not satisfied the victory is gained."[8] If Emerson's throwing up Hume to his Aunt Mary was to some extent prankish, he was taunting his own mind more than hers. He was challenging himself to transform his dissatisfaction with rational Christianity into a comprehensive inquiry into the whole rationalistic approach to knowledge. The challenge is still more insistent in another letter to her in 1824: "No fashion is so frantic as to depreciate thought. No change of times or minds has ever occurred to throw too much intellect on the market. The world is very poor amidst the rich library of all the knowledge its vaunting children have bequeathed to it. Now, in its ripe and learned old age, come I, its docile child, to be pleased and instructed by its abundant wisdom; but when I open its accepted gospels of thought and learning, its sages and bards, I find they were all fain to spin a spider web of intellect, to borrow much of each other, to arrive at a few results, and to hide or supply meagreness by profuse ornament. I am therefore curious to know what living wit (not perverted by the vulgar rage of writing a book) has suggested or concluded upon the dark sayings and sphinx riddles of philosophy and life.... Why is the fruit of knowledge sorrow? I have, it may be, a pleasant poetical cast of thought--because I am ignorant. I had a pleasanter and more romantic existence (for such is childhood) whilst I thought the rainbow a symbol and an arch in heaven, and not necessary results of light and eyes, whilst I believed that the country had more essential sacredness, some nobler difference from the town than that one was builded, t'other not. A flower and a butterfly lose every charm when poring science discloses lobes and stomachs, acids and alkalies in their delicate beauty. I dislike to augment my slender store of chemistry and astronomy, and I think I could have helped the monks to belabour Galileo for saying the everlasting earth moved. Now these lines are epitome of the history of knowledge. Every step Science has made ["science" has a more general signification here than it would have in another generation] --was it not the successive destruction of agreeable delusions which jointly made up no mean portion of human happiness? In metaphysics, 'the gymnastics of the soul,' what has reason done since Plato's day but rend and tear his gorgeous fabric. And how are we the wiser? Instead of the unmeasurable theatre which we deemed was here opened to the range of the understanding, we are now reduced to a little circle of definitions and logic round which we may humbly run. And how has faith fared? Why, the Reformer's axe has hewed down idol after idol, and corruption and imperfection, until Faith is bare and very cold. And they have not done stripping yet, but must reach the bone. The old fable said Truth was by gods or men made naked. I wish the gods would help her to a garment or make her fairer. From Eden to America the apples of the tree of knowledge are but bitter fruit in the end."[9]

We are struck by Emerson's reversal of the concept of the progress of letters. If he were merely saying that knowledge is bitter because in the form it takes in science it forces us to acknowledge that a

rainbow is a natural phenomenon and that butterflies have stomachs, we might pass over his complaint. It had become conventional by this time for poets to say that science destroys "agreeable delusions." The implication of Emerson's lament runs deeper, down indeed to the center of modern thought. In repudiating the value of accumulated knowledge and, at the same time, the triumphant movement of letters and learning from the East (Eden) to America, he indicates in his attitude toward rational knowledge that he realizes its fundamental basis in doubt. The tree of knowledge--of rational letters and learning--bears only bitter fruit, for its source of inspiration is not wonder but doubt. In The Human Condition, an erudite and imaginative explanation of the situation of modern man, Hannah Arendt points out that modern philosophy began when doubt became fully operative as a "critical method in scientific inquiry and philosophic speculation"--that is, with Descartes' de omnibus dubitandum est, with doubt conceived as the replacement of "the Greek thaumazein, the wonder of everything that is as it is." According to Arendt, "Descartes was the first to conceptualize this modern doubting, which after him became the self-evident, inaudible motor which has moved all thought, the invisible axis around which all thinking has been centered. Just as from Plato and Aristotle to the modern age conceptual philosophy, in its greatest and most authentic representations, had been the articulation of wonder, so modern philosophy since Descartes has consisted in the articulations and ramifications of doubting."[10]

In other words, with the acceptance of Cartesian doubt as the way to knowledge, Western man began to know his existence only through doubt. Emerson not only recognizes this situation but points out its origin almost explicitly when he says, "I dislike to augment my slender store of chemistry and astronomy, and I think I could have helped the monks to belabor Galileo for saying the everlasting earth moved." The idea that the earth might move was no novelty to intellect in Galileo's time. But Galileo truly disturbed the universe by making the telescope, which broke asunder forever the assumed relationship between what appears to be so and what the telescope, which sees more truly than the human eye, says is actually so. What is actually so ("the new reality") may be grasped only when the mind, refusing all that seems to be to the senses, adapts a cosmic point of view outside the world. The telescope established a cosmic standpoint, creating, Arendt says, the "new science of the Archimedean point." The ancient philosopher Archimedes dreamed of putting enough distance between himself and the world so that he could secure the leverage to lift it. As long as this kind of dream of universal power remained a dream, it had no influence on the trust in the senses and the confidence in what they reveal. Galileo's invention made it possible for the mind to act on the world from outside the world, and essentially made it necessary to doubt the validity of anything not confirmed from the Archimedean point. The world--our home--ceased to be our home and became an object of our desire to know. The cost of such detachment proved to be the loss of certainty, even the certainty that the world has an objective existence. For the senses (sight, smell, touch, hearing, taste) do not comprehend the world: it can be conceived only in the processes of cognition within the individual consciousness. There is no "given truth." Truth does not reveal itself; nothing has existence save in the constant flow of process.[11]

If young Emerson by no means explicitly comprehended all the implications of the unfolding post-Cartesianage, he was fully aware of the mood that attended the destruction of the control man had formerly had over nature when he had apprehended it through trust in his natural senses. Inherent in this trust was the power of wonder as contrasted with the power of doubt. Let me appeal to yet another entry in the Journals for 1824 (realizing that I am quoting too much but fearing not to do so lest we lost the flavor and tone--the poetry--of Emerson's thought): "To deny a Providence with Epicurus & a God with the Atheist, is a mournful speculation. It is depriving Nature of that kindly sympathy, that majestic society it held with whilst we thought it instinct with divine life. It is casting man back into a cold comfortless solitude. You leave him alone in a Universe exposed to the convulsions of disorder & the wrecks of systems where man is an atom unable to avert his peril or provide for his escape, you leave him destitute of friends who are able to control the order of Nature. While he feels himself backed by Omnipotence he can approve the nobility of his origin, can do the deeds of a godlike nature--but if you put out the Eye of the Universe, if you kill that life to which all his hopes, his virtues, his affections essentially attach themselves--that being is ruined. He thought his virtue was known & acknowledged by an omniscient & benevolent Mind; Night & Morning he lifted his hands to bless him that he had admitted him to this glorious society of intelligent beings; his heart yearned after that blissful communion which he hoped to enjoy with the Divinity--and now he learns there is no God, that virtue & vice are sick men's dreams and his heart sinks within him & hope dies. Why should he live longer in this infinite wilderness of suns & stars; he has no security, no interest, no love in dire dominion of Chance."[12]

Through the power of wonder--we may say, devising a gloss on this homily--man controlled nature by reliance on the supernatural. He was in rapport with the supernatural, himself thus godlike, in no way more so for one of Emerson's spiritual inheritance than in an intimately felt relation to Divine Providence. Underlying Emerson's reaction to atheism was not a simple, outraged response to the sacrilege of rejecting the omnipotence of God, but a complex and paradoxical response to the deprivation of man's power accompanying the loss of faith in the divine arrangement of the universe. He does not think of atheism so much as a specific philosophy as a name for the general rule of doubt, constantly expanding its sway in the eighteenth and nineteenth centuries--the bitter and novel fruit of the tree of knowledge transported into the modern world by the long progress of letters. At times he effectively put down the radical novelty of the post-Cartesian condition--vividly in 1826 in a rather lengthy meditation on the principle of compensation. Written after a very severe illness, this meditation invokes the house of the past as the proper and continuing home of the mind: "I rejoice that I live when the world is so old. There is the same difference between living with Adam and living with me as in going into a new house unfinished, damp and empty, and going into a long-occupied house where the time and taste and its inhabitants has accumulated a thousand useful contrivances, has furnished the chambers, stocked the cellars, and filled the library. In the new house every comer must do all for himself. In the old mansion there are butlers, cooks, grooms and valets. In the new house all must work, and work with the hands. In the old one there are poets who sing, actors who play and ladies who dress and smile. O ye lovers of the past, judge between my houses. I would not be elsewhere than I am."[13]

Emerson pursues his meditation into a discussion of the vanity of living for wealth and prestige. Those who do so secure their fate in "the history of retributions," which "more than any other [is] fit to establish the doctrine of Divine Providence." Not the least aspect of their destiny is that they go "unrecognized by the great brotherhood of intelligent minds who are penetrating into the obscure on every side & adding new provinces to the kingdom of knowledge."[14] This brotherhood--the community of letters and learning--Emerson says in effect is an institution of the wondrous operation of God's Providence. Thus he returns to the Christian-humanistic value system ingrained in him by inheritance. The assumed vocation of the man of letters is the fulfillment of the sense of wonder through the progressive discovery of the purpose of all things.

But the progress of the principle of doubt had entered too powerfully into Emerson's view to allow him to rest in such an assumption. If the progress of letters had become the progress of doubt, he had to find a way to break his allegiance to the received theory of the advancement of the mind in his community. Nor would a compromise with doubt, the compromise that was the rationale of Unitarianism, for long satisfy a mind so zealous for the comprehensive and the absolute as Emerson's.

In the crisis of his early thought, which was the crisis of his age, Emerson derived a great deal from Coleridge. While reading The Friend in 1829, Emerson told his Aunt Mary, "I like to encounter these citizens of the universe, that believe the mind was made to be spectator of all, inquisitor of all, and whose philosophy compares with others much as astronomy with the other sciences, taking post at the centre and, as from a specular mount, sending sovereign glances to the circumference of things."[15] This comment, with deceptive casualness, documents Emerson's initial discovery of the Archimedean point. The poet-philosopher must see into a universe in which what appears to be is no guide to what is. He must model himself on the astronomer, who has become the chief figure of the scientist. Through the instrumentation of his normal power of perception, defying the limits of the senses, the astronomer stands outside the world, taking his stand upon the Archimedean point. From this vantage point--and not merely spectator but ruthless inquisitor--he learns that all that appears to be is false, that nothing given to us by the senses is true. By means of a mind-devised instrument, his mind fabricates--his mind makes--the world and the universe, asserting the truth of concepts which quite literally repudiate what he sees without the telescope. With the telescope he becomes the Eye of the Universe.

I am exaggerating, yanking and tugging at strands in Emerson's early thought, but I think not overstating the crisis which is its basic pattern. He entered early into the anxiety of "world alienation"-- the apprehensive sense of estrangement from the earth homeland that began to arise when Galileo's ingenuity confirmed the speculation of Archimedes. If this estrangement carried in its nature the possibility of a complete and even necessary surrender to doubt, it also--before the destruction of the classical physics in the second half of the nineteenth century--offered the possibility of a freshness of wonder that seemed

comparable to Adam's in the Garden. One romantic reaction to the progress of doubt--and the institutionalization of doubt in the corporate body of letters and learning--was the assertion of the power of a faith inspired by radical novelty. When things become new again, faith makes its own forms. This would become an Emersonian dictum. "Faith," he set down in 1824, "is a telescope." He hardly grasped what he was saying, but affirmed as a metaphor of faith, instead of doubt, the telescope transformed the anxiety of alienation from the world home into a tremendous sense of phychic power. The telescope conceived poetically was a projection of the consciousness into the universe (instead of the reverse), an instrument which conferred upon man quite directly godlike capacities of perception and tantalizing prospects of universal dominion. And yet in effect the telescope was a projection of the universe into the consciousness. The dominion over the world and the universe achieved by the telescope was of the consciousness--in and of the individual consciousness so completely that, as Hannah Arendt points out, "the inner sense with which one senses his senses" is found to be the only guaranty of reality." How to be conscious of consciousness--this imperative problem makes the modern philosophers and poets into ruthless experimenters with the self. They experiment "with their own selves no less radically and perhaps even more fearlessly than the scientists have experimented with nature."[16]

On the basis of what I have attempted to set forth about the nature of the crisis in Emerson's early thought, I suppose we might say that he was from the commencement of his development as a poet and thinker irresistibly attracted to the potential power of (as Perry Miller says) "the mighty Self." This figure, the presence of which in philosophy and literature from the early nineteenth century on is so marked, we might designate with some degree of poetic license as the Archimedean Self. By the time he wrote Nature, Emerson was in the grip of a sense of amazement deriving from its daring possibilities as the omnipotent source of all knowledge. He had begun to see the traditional man of letters deriving from the concept of the "progress of letters" as useful only in the realm of the "Understanding." He already had intimations of the conviction expressed a few years later during the agitation over the Divinity School Address, when he said, "A believer, a mind whose faith is consciousness, is never disturbed because other persons do not yet see the fact which he sees."[17] In Nature he set forth an ecstatic image of the potentiality of consciousness: "Standing on the bare ground,--my head bathed by the blithe air and uplifted into infinite space,--all mean egotism vanishes. I become a transparent eyeball; I am nothing; I see all; the currents of the Universal Being circulate through me: I am part or parcel of God. The name of the nearest friend sounds then foreign and accidental: To be brothers, to be acquaintances, master or servant, is then a trifle or a disturbance. I am a lover of uncontained and immortal beauty."[18]

The famous image of the transparent eyeball--an account of a transport of wonder--is a radical metaphor of the power of the consciousness of consciousness. It represents Emerson's full apprehension of the Archimedean point conceived spiritually and poetically. The mind aware of itself comprehends all facts, and in the comprehension finds no fact monstrous. The mind reflecting on the mind is a study that never fails, a source of "perpetual revelation" (replacing historical revelation and, for that matter, the agency of Providence). In the metaphor of the transparent eyeball the issue of the crisis in Emerson's early thought is made dramatically plain: the restoration of wonder by the transforming of the radical objectivity of the rational and experimental point of view into a radically subjective or introspective one. The telescope becomes the transparent eyeball; faith is a transparent eyeball. Out of this transformation arises the novel and tremendous sense of power which excites Emerson--the capacity of the mind to transfer the universe into pure vision and, thus locating it in the mind, to control and direct it. This capacity is what Emerson in his retrospective "Life and Letters in New England" terms the "new consciousness." (It is the response he made to the necessity of finding a "new reality" to replace the "old reality" lost through the separation of Being and Appearance.) In Nature the enraptured "contemplation of the whole"--that is to say, "the wonder at everything that is as it is"--is restored. At least it would seem to be restored. In this vision one can again exist in a pre-Cartesian (and pre-Christian) unity and harmony with the All, no longer threatened by estrangement from Being, the lover of "uncontained and immortal beauty."

But there are other implications in Emerson's exuberant vision of consciousness, which he did not grasp, though they haunted him and are reflected in the decline of his spiritual arrogance in the 1840's, when he came to recognize that vision is mediate and that the mind cannot look upon the mind. Ironically, the expense of being a lover of transcendent beauty is essentially the same one imposed upon the disciple of doubt. It is alienation from the world homeland of man and the community of men who make the world a household. Implied in the godlike capacity of controlling the universe as a transparent eyeball is not only

an aspiration to the dimensionless character of God and the denial of any fixity of time and space, but the desertion of the community of human relationships. Family, friends, servants--all fade as the Self in the flow of the currents of the Universal Being becomes part and parcel of God. The flow of Being is away from the human community of the world and never toward it. There is no returning stream. In 1838 Emerson had his most ecstatic, austere, and chilling vision of the destiny of the Self: "The things we now esteem fixed shall, one by one, detach themselves like ripe fruit from our experience, and fall. The wind shall blow them none knows whither. The landscape, the figures, Boston, London, are facts as fugitive as any institution past, or any whiff of mist or smoke, and so is the world. The soul looketh steadily forwards, creating a world before her, leaving worlds behind her. She has no dates, nor rites, nor persons, nor specialities, nor men. The soul knows only the soul; the web of events is the flowing robe in which she is clothed."[19]

Believing explicitly in the ultimate morality of all things and in the absolute moral character of the consciousness that is the soul, Emerson contemplated the wonder of sheer Becoming--the infinite progress of consciousness from that mere fugitive fact, the world--as the perfection of knowledge that came with "the action of man upon nature with his entire force,--with reason as well as understanding." He was willing to accept, in states of ecstasy at any rate, the consequence of the progress of consciousness, which is the utter loss of the human world. So Emerson followed the logic of the moral analogy he saw between faith and the telescope; never, however, clearly discerning its precarious nature. The uncontained and immortal beauty he dared to love and the solitudes of space Pascal feared share a common source--alienation from the household of the world originating in the action of the mind upon nature from a perspective outside that which shaped man's sense of actuality before Galileo. Without the moral and mystical assumptions of Emerson, the control of man over nature is open to the ruthless, merciless, dehumanizing exploitation of the world that has attended its perception from the "specular mount" of ceaseless doubt. The technological desecration of a great symbol of wonder like the moon is only the latest testimony to the failure of Emerson's heroic attempt to restore wonder to its ancient place in the modern psyche.

Louisiana State University

1 For information on the experiences of poverty, illness, and death in Emerson's early life, see the following: Ralph L. Rusk, The Life of Ralph Waldo Emerson (N.Y., 1944), pp. 1-151; The Letters of Ralph Waldo Emerson (N.Y., 1939), Vol. I; The Journals and Miscellaneous Notebooks of Ralph Waldo Emerson, edited by William H. Gilman and others (Cambridge, 1960-), Vols. I, II; The Journals of Ralph Waldo Emerson, edited by Edward Waldo Emerson and Waldo Emerson Forbes (Boston and N.Y., 1911-1914), Vols. I, II. The nature of the New England clerisy is discussed in Lewis P. Simpson, "Joseph Stevens Buckminster and the New England Clerisy," an essay in a volume of the Louisiana State University Studies in the Humanities scheduled for publication in the spring, 1970. Also, see The Federalist Literary Mind, edited by Lewis P. Simpson (Baton Rouge, 1962). 2 JMN, II, 232.
3 Quoted in Benjamin T. Spencer, The Quest for Nationality (Syracuse, 1957), p. 22.
4 Monthly Anthology and Boston Review, IV (November, 1807), 600. 5 JMN, II, 231.
6 Ibid., II, 140-141. 7 Ibid. 8 Letters, I, 137-138. 9 Journals, I, 374-377.
10 My indebtedness to Hannah Arendt, The Human Condition (N.Y., 1959) is general in this essay. See especially pp. 225ff.
11 See ibid., especially 234ff. 12 JMN, II, 252. 13 Ibid., II, 340.
14 Ibid., II, 342. Cf. Sheldon W. Liebman, "Emerson's Transformation in the 1820's," American Literature, XL (May, 1968), 133-154. This excellent essay reflects the scholarly preoccupation with Emerson's Unitarianism. It attempts to narrow the explanation of Emerson's transformation to his temperament, but, I think, not convincingly. 15 Journals, II, 277. 16 The Human Condition, p. 267.
17 Selections from Ralph Waldo Emerson, ed. Stephen E. Whicher (Boston, 1957), p. 119.
18 Ibid., p. 24. 19 Ibid., p. 93.

EMERSON'S "INSTANT ETERNITY": AN EXISTENTIAL APPROACH

MARY EDRICH REDDING

In Nature, frustrated in his attempt to reconcile the worlds of mind and matter, Emerson finally offered a metaphor rather than a philosophically sound reconciliation: he described the world as "one vast

picture which God paints on the instant eternity for the contemplation of the soul."[1] Modern heirs of existentialism are able to live comfortably with such a failure of formal philosophy, and Emerson himself often maintained that philosophic systems do not afford understanding of existence, which is not logical but real: "Metaphysics teach me admirably well what I knew before; setting out in order particular after particular, bone after bone, the anatomy of the mind. My knowledge is thus arranged [,] not augmented.... But neither metaphysics nor ethics are more than outside sciences. They give me no insight into the nature & design of my being."[2] But we must note that "pictures"--or metaphors--can be as misleading as logical symbols if they are offered or interpreted as conveying in themselves a reliable structure by means of which man can relate to the world--can overcome alienation.

Martin Buber has described this alienation and the futility of man's effort to resolve it with constructs not very different in kind from Emerson's "vast picture." Buber explains how "Self-Contradiction" (alienation) occurs: "If a man does not represent the a priori of relation in his living with the world, if he does not work out and realize the inborn Thou on what meets it, then it strikes inwards.... Thus confrontation of what is over against him takes place within himself, and this cannot be relation, or presence, or streaming interaction, but only self-contradiction. The man may seek to explain it as a relation, perhaps as a religious relation, in order to wrench himself from the horror of the inner double-ganger; but he is bound to discover again and again the deception in the explanation. Here is the verge of life, flight of an unfulfilled life to the senseless semblance of fulfillment."[3] At times this man will realize his own alienation from the world, Buber states, and will call "thought" to his aid: "It is, in truth, the high art of thought to paint a reliable picture of the world that is even worthy of belief." Then Buber proceeds to demonstrate that eventually these pictures will cease to put man at ease and that an even deeper awareness of alienation will overcome him.[4] In "Illusions," Emerson confesses his own abortive attempt to "paint away" dread: "...if Marmaduke, or Hugh, or Moosehead, or any other, invent a new style or mythology, I fancy the world will be all brave and right if dressed in these colors, which I had not thought of. Then at once I will daub with this new paint; but it will not stick" (W, VI, 316-317).

The tendency to deal with alienation in terms of constructs rather than from authenticity is dramatically evident in mid-twentieth-century America. Today we mistake selfishness for authenticity; and, with equal self-deception, smugly account for alienation by pointing our fingers at externals. We sociologize, pretending that alienation is altogether the result of environmental problems rather than the cause of them. To take a familiar example, a supposedly civilized man who can kill helpless babies in a battle-zone is able to do so not because war has taught him to be inhuman, but because he does not see these babies as human beings to begin with. In short, he creates the war in his individual act of atrocity. Where the self-deception begins is in the individual. So it is from examining a form of self-deception in the writings of a man who desperately sought to avoid self-deception that we can most learn. Since we are dangerously close to "bad-faith" in our using Buber's statements as standards by which to determine the authenticity of Emerson, we must avoid making facile assumptions about Emerson's genuine struggle with the universe. But it will be rewarding to place these men of two centuries, who were so similar, into relationship with one another, that we may witness the authenticity of their concerns.

As Buber states, the experience of confrontation "cannot be taught in the sense of precepts given. It can only be indicated by the drawing of a circle which excludes everything that is not this going out. Then the one thing that matters is visible, full acceptance of the present." This acceptance "does not mean a giving up of...the I, as mystical writings usually suppose...since relation is only possible between I and Thou." What is given up is "that false self-asserting instinct that makes a man flee to the possessing of things before the unreliable, perilous world of relation which has neither density nor duration and cannot be surveyed."[5]

Emerson devoted his life to lamenting the domination of men by the "things" to which the perilous world of relation so often drove them; yet, ironically, his struggle led him along a similar path at times. The perilousness which pursued him was mortality; the "things" were the philosophic constructs by which he sought to reassure himself. His demand for authenticity took many forms: he saw in the passion of the ancient Hebrews and that of his Puritan predecessors a piety preferable to the "Bare reason, cold as cucumber" which still had advocates in his own day,[6] and he rejected the use of miracles to buy allegiance where true faith was lacking. In his own case, a sense of personal responsibility would not permit him to settle for easy promises of redemption or immortality. But his authenticity was attenuated so long as he saw too

much value in philosophic idealism to avoid imitating its cognitive reliance upon structure. Kurt Reinhardt has explained: "German idealists proposed to get rid of the troublesome concrete subject by immersing it in a 'general consciousness' (Kant) or in an absolute, universal ego (Fichte, Hegel)," whereas authenticity involves risk, a junction of opposites, and a dynamic subjectivity on the part of the concrete human being.[7] For the existentialist, as for Kierkegaard, the "authentically human factor is passion."[8] We shall now consider how Emerson drew away from the passionate inwardness of his reaction to the existence of death and how he developed what became an increasingly structured definition of immortality.

Young Emerson's philosophical concern with immortality emanated from an intense need for personal reassurance. Afflicted with ill health, surrounded by death, he longed to know that he deserved to survive. "I am sick--if I should die what would become of me [?]" he wrote in 1821. "I must improve my time better. I must prepare myself for the great profession I have proposed to undertake. I am to give my soul to God & withdraw from sin & the world the idle or vicious time & thoughts I have sacrificed to them" (JMN, I, 52). At times resorting to a kind of wishful thinking, he virtually invested his placebo--hope of immortality--with a reality of its own. "Hope, which is God's voice and prophecy--of a better state beyond the grave," Emerson described as man's "chief happiness," without which man would be a "miserable monument of divine vengeance" and the world "a blank & rotteness."[9] His choice of consolation was significant. Characteristically, when driven into a corner of gloom, he tried to recover himself by drawing upon the stoic consolation that a man's frame of mind is the determining factor in how he is to resolve a difficulty. Yet young Emerson moved beyond stoicism in his attributing to frame of mind almost talismanic powers: "We are reduced to put our views of death entirely upon...[God's] character & will, and Death will become more or less terrible according to our notions of the lord of Death" (JMN, I, 109). In truth his history is a biography of faith's ups and downs. In 1822, he wrote, "Hope it is true, still hangs out, though at further distance, her gay banners; but I have found her a cheat once, twice, many times, and shall I trust the deceiver again?" (JMN, I, 130).

There is little indication that Emerson ever took very seriously the New Testament assurance of salvation through Christ. The very fact that he referred to Jesus so seldom before 1825[10] indicates his preference for direct confrontation with God. Inspired by the example of Milton--who had presumed to tackle God in his own theodicy, young Emerson began to agonize over questions of human depravity, God's benevolence, the imputation of Adam's guilt, and the educative aspect of sin.[11] He never intellectually questioned the right of God to afflict men, insisting that the "Being who created can destroy.... Annihilation is a prerogative of God" (JMN, II, 66). He did, however, attempt to reconcile the justice of this affliction with his need as a Christian to conceive of God as benevolent. The stumbling-block was the Old Testament portrayal of the God of wrath.[12] While youthful Emerson could assert, "Turn ye [,] turn ye [,] for why will ye die? It will not be the fault of God nor of his prophets & priests" (JMN, II, 129), the young widower would find totally inapplicable the Calvinistic vision of God smiting dead the hardened sinner.

Even before entering the Divinity School, Emerson had gone through the motions of rejecting the Calvinism which had so invaded his thought;[13] yet he was drawing himself up to the gates of Unitarianism with no little discomfiture. His task now was to sort out the mélange of religious ties which had hitherto constituted his vague and often paradoxical spiritual inheritances, and to become the exponent of a particular sect. The task would be difficult for one who was beginning to question the existential validity of systems. He remarked, "Men's creeds can never, at least in youth, set the heart entirely at east. They strike the eye ever & anon as fine spun textures through which rebellious doubt is impatient, sometimes desperate, to plunge" (JMN, II, 244). In any case he was willing to concentrate upon alignment: "If I devote my nights & days in form, to the service of God & the War against Sin, --I shall soon be prepared to do the same in substance" (JMN, II, 241). These forms of the church and of old rhetoric rules were to be discarded by Emerson with sigh of relief in the early 1830's, but not until he had given the New Testament a conventional ministerial emphasis in his sermons.

That he should have even attempted to become a minister, knowing what conformity would be demanded of him, might seem incomprehensible were it not for his admiration for Dr. William Ellery Channing, whose thought had offered what must have been a temptingly optimistic view of immortality. Channing denied hell, calling it a "metaphor" which "has done unspeakable injury to Christianity." He afforded instead a "religion which aims to attract and assimilate us to God."[14] More consistently confident of man's stature and worth than Emerson would ever be, Channing rarely succumbed to the painful Pascal-like

broodings which can be found throughout Emerson's writings: "We are of that feeble frame that every accident threatens our being, the wound of a pin will let out our life; a fever, a humour, a draft of cold air will destroy it, and put a final period to all our intercourse with men, all our repentance, our perseverance, our enthusiasm, our faith, our hope on earth."[15] Channing promised that although heaven was not a "mere place," it was a "union of spirit" among men and God, and he stressed the fact that it is upon virtuous living that immortality depends.[16]

With respect to this matter of the conduct of life Emerson's attachment to certain Old Testament themes took precedence over the Old Testament-permeated Calvinistic emphasis of his youth. Whereas Calvinism rejected the notion that "good works" have any effect upon one's attaining immortality, the Old Testament dramatized the idea that if some are chosen, nevertheless all must live productively; to live well is to fulfill the requirements for a long life and for tribal recognition, as witnessed by the longevity of the Hebrew Patriarchs. Sometime around 1825, Emerson observed that the "Jewish philosopher did not know that the soul survived the body yet there seemed to him a peculiar sympathy & conjunction between vice & death and the idea was natural & suggests the evidence we have from nature of the immortality of the soul.... Since virtue was imperishable every act contrary to it would seem to tend to the destruction of the agent.--Vice is the soul's suicide."[17] And in May, 1838, he expressed what was to be a central idea in both the Divinity School address and "Compensation:" "Learn that the malignity &...lie of the wrongdoer are the shadows of death creeping over him; that so far is he deceasing from nature; that in a virtuous action I properly am; in a virtuous act I expend myself into real nature, & see the darkness...receding the limits of the horizon" (JMN, V, 493). The relating of good to real being, and evil to chaos and non-being, goes back to Genesis, where God creates the universe by subduing "tohu" and "bohu" (chaos and void). We find Buber making the same comparison: "'Good' is the movement in the direction of home, 'evil' is the aimless whirl of human potentialities without which nothing can be achieved and by which, if they take no direction but remain trapped in themselves, everything goes awry."[18]

Moreover, the Hebraic "tooth for a tooth" concept of justice, translated into a "pay as you go" emphasis by the American genius, became central to the "instant rewards and punishment" concept of the theory of compensation which Emerson had begun to develop during his school-teaching days (1823-1825). As Roland F. Lee has pointed out, Emerson's doctrine of compensation is a violation of Emerson's own dismay over those who take creeds or intellectual classifications for ends in themselves rather than for temporary means.[19]

By 1827, Emerson could inform his aunt that he rejected the idea of a future world as the place of final moral reward, and, three years later, could note with interest that Sampson Reed's "new faith teaches him not to regard...[death] as a punishment." "It is in being good to wife & children that the kingdom of heaven begins," Emerson affirmed in 1832; "we should not fabricate a heaven in our heads & then square life to that fiction." Doing one's duty and spending each hour well constitute immortality.[20]

His emphasis upon the obligations of the Now and upon living--an emphasis inherent in Hebrew tradition absorbed from the Bible and fortified by his mentor, Dr. Channing--found passing support from still a third source: Thomas Carlyle. In 1833, Emerson, referring to his Craigenputtock meeting, noted Carlyle's belief in the "merely relative existence of Time & hence his faith in his immortality."[21] And, on November 5, 1836, Carlyle offered a bereaved Emerson the consolation that his loved ones "are in Eternity, which is a Now and Here"--a concept echoed by Emerson one month later: "Yet they ask me whether I know the soul immortal. No. But do I not know the now to be eternal?"[22]

The relevance of both the Hebraic and the existential aspects of the infinitude of the Now receives this testimony from Buber: "Actually...pure relation can only be raised to constancy in space and time by being embodied in the whole stuff of life.... Man can do justice to the relation with God in which he has come to share only if he realizes God anew in the world according to his strength and to the measure of each day. In this lies the only authentic assurance of continuity."[23] Nor did Emerson intend to deny the existential quality of the everyday world or the personal aspects of everyday experience: his desire to raise men "out of the finite into the infinite; out of time into eternity" reflected more an objection to "the exclusive commerce with outward things" as objects than an unwillingness to see the eternal in the everyday.[24] Herbert Schneider goes even further and concludes that Emerson is existential rather than phenomenological because his "seeing all things in personal perspective is not a mental structure that is imposed

on an alien world; it is a practical philosophy.... His building of his own world in poetic imagination is at the same time his practical appropriation of the real world."[25] Emerson insisted, "I do not wish to exchange the idea of immortality against that of the beatitude of one day" (W, VIII, 330).

Even as "eternity, in the Hebraic view, is not escape from, but fulfillment of time," and is "now"--as well as hereafter--"because, in fellowship with God, all the vicissitudes of time are overcome and transcended,"[26] so too in Emerson does eternity take place intensively rather than merely chronologically or as a measurable immeasurability: "Future state is an illusion for the ever-present state. It is not length of life but depth of life." He explained in "Immortality:" "It is not duration, but a taking of the soul out of time, as all high action of the mind does" (W, VIII, 347). Thus, for Emerson, "Life only avails, not the having lived.... The soul becomes" (W, II, 69).[27] The goal is not an afterworld but development in this world.

To approach the problem of how the soul was to become, Emerson eclectically fell back upon elements from Calvinistic, Platonic, Prophetical, and Miltonic traditions, and unwittingly began to contrive the system which eventually vitiated his confidence in immortality. As he conceived it, the soul--needing "redemption"[28] (the Calvinistic element)--must strive for a higher state (the Platonic) by attending to the inner messages and promptings of the divine (the Prophetical). To render oneself fit for receiving and celebrating these messages, one must live chastely (the Miltonic): "The body which we inhabit shall shortly be laid in the dust, but the soul assures us, with the voice of God to confirm it, that it will not die.... Let us leave this immoderate regard to meats and drinks, to dress and pleasure and to unfounded praise, and let us go alone and converse with ourselves, and the word of God in us."[29]

Although Emerson's God was not personal enough to prevent his concept of immortality from becoming a rather cold intellectual abstraction, he must have valued this dialogue aspect of the personal relationship between God and the Hebrew prophets and patriarchs.[30] It was reasonable for Emerson, a man of letters, to envision a man-God relationship based upon communication. The problem of authenticity arises when Emerson uses this relationship as a "thing"--as a structure for establishing immortality. This "using" the I-Thou dialogue is referred to by Buber: "He who has been converted by this substitution of object now 'holds' a phantom that he calls God. But God, the eternal Presence, does not permit Himself to be held. Woe to the man so possessed that he thinks he possesses God!"[31] The similarity between Emerson's view of poetic inspiration and Buber's I-Thou dialogue is nevertheless apparent in Buber's discussion of Hölderlin, "who understood poetry as the combined work of the inspiring gods and the men inspired by them."[32] On a more basic level, we perceive the likeness of the discussion of language in Nature to Buber's assertion, "in God's response everything, the universe, is made manifest as language."[33]

An idiosyncratic or selfish individualism never truly appealed to Emerson, who asked: "Are there not moments in the history of heaven when the human race was not counted by individuals, but was only the Influenced, was God in distribution, God rushing into multiform benefit? It is sublime to receive, sublime to love, but this lust of imparting as from us, this desire to be loved, the wish to be recognized as individuals--is finite, comes of a lower strain" (W, I, 210). Buber makes a similar distinction between the "person" and the "individual:" "The person looks on his Self, individuality is concerned with its My.... Individuality neither shares in nor obtains any reality. It differentiates itself from the other, and seeks through experiencing and using to appropriate as much of it as it can."[34] In Emerson too we find some of the Hebraic insistence that human personality is realized only through its finding "a secure grounding in the eternal Person that is ultimate reality."[35] In fact this insistence was virtually all that enabled Emerson to remain a theist. The transmission of moral information from the Greater Being to the lesser--man--marked the dependency of the latter upon the former: "All writing comes by the grace of God," Emerson proclaimed; "The poet works to an end above his will, and by means, too, which are out of his will" (W, XII, 71). Elsewhere, he again observes of the poet: "By and by he says something which is original and beautiful.... But the poet knows well that it is not his.... Once having tasted this immortal ichor he cannot have enough of it" (W, III, 39).

Emerson's description of the process by which such communication takes place has an apocalyptic ring: "Man is a stream whose source is hidden...from some alien energy the visions come" (W, II, 268). One recalls the loneliness of the prophets who reluctantly sacrificed themselves to become vehicles for God's word: "The soul gives itself, alone, original and pure, to the Lonely, Original, and Pure, who, on

that condition, gladly inhabits, leads and speaks through it" (W, II, 296). At last, the prophetic career must end: "The god of bounds" addresses the poet, instructing him to "no more invent," but to "Contract" his "firmament - To compass of a tent" (W, IX, 251). As a symbol, the tent (which in "Threnody" is "a traveller's fleeing tent" and a metaphor for heaven: W, IX, 157) calls to mind the house of the holy ark transported by the wandering children of Israel, the vehicle of the Divine truth bestowed upon them.

However emotionally unsettled his concept of immortality left Emerson, intellectually the transmission of truth to man's soul was assumed by him to be a cure for "the taint of mortality."[37] In 1838, he wrote: "Nature insures herself.... She makes a man & having brought him to ripe old age she will no longer run the risk of losing this wonder at a blow, but she detaches from him a new self that the work may be safe from the accidents to which the single individual is exposed. So when the Soul of the poet has come to the ripeness of thought it detaches from itself & sends away from it its poems or songs, a fearless, sleepless, deathless progeny which is not exposed to the accidents of the weary kingdom of time" (JMN, VII, 87-88). "In Heaven, utterance is place enough," he observed in 1835. "It is, as Coleridge said, another world but not to come. The world I describe is that, where...only the laws of the mind are known, the only economy of time is saying & doing nothing untrue to self" (JMN, V, 48). And, in 1838, he wrote: "Our thought is the income of God. I taste therefore of eternity & pronounce of eternal law now & not hereafter. Space & time are but forms of thought. I proceed from God now & ever shall so proceed. Death is but an appearance" (JMN, V, 499).

Nor was Emerson's assumption that immortality depends upon a momentary Divine communication a part of this thought only after he had become a man of letters. As early as 1826, he wrote to his aunt: "...it is one of the feelings of modern philosophy, that it is wrong to regard ourselves so much in a historical light as we do, putting Time between God and us; and that it were fitter to account every moment of the existence of the Universe as a new Creation, and all as a revelation proceeding each moment from the Divinity to the mind of the observer" (L, I, 174). And, in 1827, he rejoiced in the "heyday of youth when time is marked not by numbering days but by the intervals of mentality the flux & reflux of the soul" (L, I, 191). The writer in Emerson was already beginning to see poetry as an antidote to feelings of mortality.[38]

In 1832, Emerson, mourning the death of his wife, had an additional consolation derived from conceiving of an immortality based upon Divine communication. On January 27, he wrote: "Talked with Reed & Worcester last ev'g.... God, we agreed, was the communication between us & other spirits departed or present" (JMN, III, 324). "Oh what is Heaven but the fellowship / Of minds...?" he poetized two years later (JMN, IV, 341).

Needless to say, Emerson's idea of an immortality inherent in man's dutifully receiving Divine communications in the Here and the Now often failed to satisfy. The purpose in viewing immortality as a happening in life itself was to render the concept more existentially meaningful--more "alive;" yet, as we have stated, Emerson over-structured his concept until it became a total abstraction. Cliches are apropos of existential experience so long as they do not become constricting labels or definitions of experience; hence as a cliche only the platitude that a poet's immortality is his poetry might have sufficed. Certainly Emerson could not have asked too much of such a concept in any given instance. But, for him, the instant was the eternity, an eternity to the degree that language (Divine inspiration) took place. Language did not always happen, and on one such occasion--doubly threatened by his temporary loss of artistic power and his temporary default of immortality--he asserted: "Gladly I would solve if I could this problem of a Vocabulary which like some treacherous wide shoal waylays the tall bark [,] the goodly soul & there it founders & suffers shipwreck.... Every man is lobsided [sic] and even holding in his hands some authentic token & gift of God holds it awry" (JMN, VII, 149). "The ancients strongly expressed their sense of the unmanageableness of these words of the God, by saying that the God made his priest insane...took him hither & thither as leaves are whirled by the tempest. But," he concluded, "we sing as we are bid" (JMN, VII, 267).

The greatest insufficiency in his concept of immortality was not so evident in its application to himself or to humanity as a whole. When it had to apply to other particular individuals it especially failed to comfort. Ellen's modest poems somehow fell short of the "immortal ichor" of the divinely inspired. His brothers' talents had also reached only limited development and were modest in achievement. Most agonizing for Emerson to bear was the silencing of his tiny son: "For flattering planets seemed to say / This

child should ills of ages stay, / By wondrous tongue, and guided pen, / Bring the flown Muses back to men" (W, IX, 153). The lad, whose "lips could well pronounce / Words that were persuasions" (W, IX, 150) was not to live long enough to celebrate truths imparted divinely in the instant eternity.

Approaching the same poem as art, we might reverse Buber's statement that "In the work of art realization in one sense means loss of reality in another,"[39] and point out that the very disparity in Emerson's view of immortality gave contrast and depth to this as to many of his works. In "Threnody," the tension between the intellectualized grief of the artificial and conventional expressions ("air's cerulean round," "hyacinthine boy," "Morn well might break," and so forth) and the genuine existentially spontaneous experiencing of grief in the recollections of the details of Waldo's play, habits, and mannerisms, intensifies the psychological impact of the poem as neither a confident philosophy of immortality nor a completely unabashed pouring forth of passion could ever have done. Emerson at times seems to mock his own intellections:

> I gave thee sight--where is it now?
> I taught thy heart beyond the reach
> Of ritual, bible, or of speech;
> Wrote in thy mind's transparent table,
> As far as the incommunicable;
> (W, IX, 155).

Here Emerson confesses that his concept of immortality-as-communication has failed its existential purpose--has become merely mechanical. He laments "truth's and nature's costly lie," and the "trusted broken prophecy;" and admits the total inadequacy of language[40] as a mode of expressing his grief--the mocking rhythm of the verse indicating his own impatience with his words: "Nature, who lost, cannot remake him; / Fate let him fall, Fate can't retake him; / Nature, Fate, men, him seek in vain" (W, IX, 149). Frustrated by the limitations of words, Emerson suggests the dimensions of his pain only in the understated "I am too much bereft" (p. 154) and by existentially living out his grief through references to the sights and sounds of his environment before and after Waldo's death:

> On that shaded day,
> Dark with more clouds than tempests are,
> When thou didst yield thy innocent breath
> In birdlike heavings unto death....
> The morrow dawned with needless glow;
> Each snowbird chirped, each fowl must
> crow;
> (W, IX, 151).

If in "Threnody" Emerson is often parodying what he perhaps now sees as his former philosophic smugness, he nevertheless concludes that poem on what appears to be a note of confidence: "Lost in God, in Godhead found." But here Godhead seems to be less a statement of the immortality of the human spirit absorbed into the Source of all spirit than a resigning oneself to the forces of nature--rather like that of Wordsworth's "A Slumber Did My Spirit Seal." Heaven is now "a nest of bending reeds" (perhaps inspired by Pascal's describing man as a "thinking reed")--a setting where frail man may enact his dignity by "furtherance and pursuing." With his admission that heaven is "Built of tears" as well as of "sacred flames," Emerson and his grief became one (W, IX, 157-158).

They did not remain so. Emerson was unable to dispel that despair which is "sickness unto death," and for which Kierkegaard offers his own formula for faith: "By relating itself to its own self and by willing to be itself, the self is grounded transparently in the Power which constituted it."[41] Emerson's depersonalizing God virtually into a cold abstraction will suffice in part to explain his despair. He was aware that our notion of God must determine the nature of our views of death (JMN, I, 109) and that one must "cleave to God against the name of God" (W, XII, 6); but there was never for Emerson the passionateness of the encounter with the Other which forms the strength of Buber's faith. While the Divinity School address statement, "The man who renounces himself, comes to himself" (W, I, 122) suggests a giving of oneself to the Other, it is more clearly an avowal that by renouncing petty individuality and selfish egotism, one comes to an awareness of one's universal moral nature. Emerson's Hebraic unwillingness to invest his God with anthropomorphic traits was, perhaps unfortunately for his own love of piety, carried to such an extreme form of depersonalization that on one occasion he could assert, "When I speak of God, I prefer to say It--It."[42] It is one's temperament which gets in the way, Emerson explains truthfully in "Experience:" "Temperament puts all divinity to rout" (W, III, 52).

As a confession of his own problems in achieving what in Buber is the I-Thou relationship, Emerson's essay "Experience" is a veritable casebook of what lies outside the I-Thou "circle:" "Life is not

dialectics," "It is very unhappy, but too late to be helped, the discovery we have made that we exist" (i.e., that we live as objects among objects). "Gladly we would anchor, but the anchorage is quicksand."[43] He concludes the essay on a note of quiet understanding rather than of confident joy: "I know that the world I converse with in the city and in the farms is not the world I think.... One day I shall know the value and law of this discrepance. But I have not found that much was gained by manipular attempt to realize the world of thought." "Patience and patience, we shall win at the last" (W, III, 84-85).

As antidotes to fate, Emerson cites the intellectual ("thought") and the universal ethical ("moral sentiment"), but dilutes the confrontation of what is over against him (in the experience of which he admits he "cannot look without seeing splendor and grace") when he intellectually translates it into "the necessity of beauty under which the universe lies; that all is and must be pictorial"--"the central intention of Nature to be harmony and joy."[44] Similarly, in "Illusions," he urges authenticity (W, VI, 322-323) and claims, "We see God face to face every hour, and know the savor of nature" (p. 324). But when it comes time for him to reveal the relationship between man and gods--"they alone with him alone"--he introduces the paragraph containing a description of this encounter with a "structure:" "There is no chance and anarchy in the universe. All is system and gradation. Every god is there sitting in his sphere" (p. 325).

If in Emerson's inability to achieve authenticity in his encounter with mortality one factor was his sacrificing the personal to the intellectual relationship with God, a second factor of equal significance was his translating the sincerely personal meaning which others had for himself into allegories of the "spiritual system." "Grief makes us idealists," he generalizes in "Experience;" then he proceeds to wonder that "grief can teach...[him] nothing, nor carry...[him] one step into real nature" (W, III, 48-49)! Small wonder that Stephen E. Whicher responded to Emerson's moralizing over his young wife's death, with the exclamation, "The hardness of the saints!"[45]

Emerson gives evidence that he knows better than to make objects of others, when he cautions: "Let us treat the men and women well; treat them as if they were real; perhaps they are" (W, III, 60). For Buber it is Love which "comes to pass" and in which a man dwells, rather than feelings which are "entertained" and which dwell in a man, that enables one to see others as real: "In the eyes of him who takes his stand in love, and gazes out of it..." all people--"Good people and evil, wise and foolish, beautiful and ugly, become successively real to him; that is, set free they step forth in their singleness, and confront him as Thou."[46] Inevitably, Buber admits, and no "matter how exclusively present the Thou was in the direct relation," every Thou must become an It: "Genuine contemplation is over in a short time; now the life in nature, that first unlocked itself to me in the mystery of mutual action, can again be described, taken to pieces, and classified--the meeting-point of manifold systems of laws."[47] We have already noted a passage in Emerson's essay "Experience," which indicates an awareness that our seeing ourselves as objects among objects is the true "Fall of Man" (W, III, 75).

We have perceived that because of his anxiety over death and the intellectual oversimplifications to which he clung in the face of this anxiety he experienced a spiritual encounter which was in many ways merely partial and negative, but never entirely so. After listing the various labels for God--"Fortune, Minerva, Muse, Holy Ghost"--and observing that these individual "metaphors" had each become a "national religion," he admitted the inadequacy of his own label: "In our more correct writing we give to this generalization the name of Being, and thereby confess that we have arrived as far as we can go." He nevertheless rejoiced that "we have not arrived at a wall, but at interminable oceans. Our life seems not present so much as prospective" (W, III, 72-73). In his prospective he is aware in a very practical way that there is much for man to be doing and much for him to experience. Buber is more specific: "This is the ultimate purpose: to let God in. But we can let him in only where we really stand, where we live, where we live a true life."[48] For Emerson, too, the prospect is still faith: "...it is not what we believe concerning the immortality of the soul or the like, but the universal impulse to believe, that is the material circumstance and is the principal fact in the history of the globe" (p. 74). Here, and wherever he attributes less importance to the content of belief and greater importance to the experiential impulse to believe, he takes his place among the existential thinkers.

From the vantage-point of the twentieth century, we perceive that although in Emerson are met the two polar approaches of nineteenth-century thought--the cognitive and the existential--it was in large measure the effectiveness of his existential approach to meaning which inspired his followers. The superb

intellectual gymnastics behind the carefully calculated rhetorical structures of Walden should not be confused with the existential encounter implicit in Thoreau's paradoxes or in his often negative, yet personal, search for authenticity. For Whitman more completely than for any other Emerson-inspired writer, the search for an I-Thou relationship came to pass--most directly in "To You, Whoever You Are" and in his responding to flowers and animals; but most poignantly in his "Wound-dresser's" understanding that he cannot spare his young companions the often grievous passionate inwardness of experience, for--as Kierkegaard states--"Whatever the one generation may learn from the other, that which is genuinely human no generation learns from the foregoing.... This authentically human factor is passion."[49]

It is not the passion itself, then, but the acceptance of the authenticity of passion that we learn from others. If Emerson's structures--his doctrine of compensation, his concept of immortality, and some of his metaphors--strike us as the very "pasteboard and filigree" which he decried in the Divinity School address (W, I, 150), we find a more haunting challenge in his warning: "Whatever games are played with us, we must play no games with ourselves, but deal in our privacy with the last honesty and truth" (W, VI, 322).

San Diego State College

---

1 The Complete Works of Ralph Waldo Emerson, ed. Edward Waldo Emerson, 12 vols. (Boston and N.Y., 1903-1904), I, 69. Subsequent references to this edition will be designated "W".
2 The Journals and Miscellaneous Notebooks of Ralph Waldo Emerson, ed. William H. Gilman, et al., 7 vols. (Cambridge, Mass., 1960-1969), II, 245. A scholar who especially understands some of the existential aspects of Emerson's thought is Roland F. Lee: "Emerson Through Kierkegaard: Toward a Definition of Emerson's Theory of Communication," ELH, XXIV (September, 1957), 229-248.
3 I and Thou, 2nd ed. (N.Y., 1958), p. 70. 4 Ibid., pp. 70-72. 5 Ibid., pp. 77-78.
6 The Letters of Ralph Waldo Emerson, ed. Ralph L. Rusk, 6 vols. (N.Y., 1939), I, 174. Subsequent references to this edition will be designated "L".
7 Kurt F. Reinhardt, The Existentialist Revolt, 2nd ed. (N.Y., 1960), p. 17.
8 Soren Kierkegaard, Fear and Trembling and The Sickness Unto Death, tr. Walter Lowrie (Garden City, 1954), p. 130.
9 JMN, II, 61; I, 185; II, 163. See Mary Edrich [Redding], Emerson's Apostasy, an unpublished dissertation (Univ. of Wisconsin, 1965), pp. 107-111; and Henry F. Pommer, Emerson's First Marriage (Carbondale and Edwardsville, 1967), p. 119, note 77. Pommer is correct in stating that an emphasis on hope can be found in Emerson as early as 1830. The passages cited in this footnote are from 1821-1823.
10 The Journals indicate that most of Emerson's references to Jesus occur after he had moved to Roxbury where he began his independent study for the ministry. Pommer states that in 1829, "Emerson preached 'the Resurrection from the Dead' and Jesus as promising immortality" (p. 76). However, it is by no means clear from the text of that sermon that Emerson actually believed in either, but merely that he and his parishioners would converse and reflect on them. See Young Emerson Speaks, ed. Arthur C. McGiffert, Jr. (Boston, 1938), pp. 34-35. Subsequent references to this edition will be designated "YES". Emerson's letter to Henry Ware, Jr. (July 1, 1829) is also inconclusive; he states merely that he considers the Scriptures to be "the true record of the Revelation which established what was almost all we wanted to know, namely the Immortality of the Soul" (L, I, 273).
11 See JMN, I, 173; II, 88-89, 115, 56, 64; I, 93, 312-313, 350-351; I, 187, 108, 57. Emerson, in 1822, spoke of himself as "Anxious to...vindicate the ways of God to man" (Ibid., I, 313).
12 See JMN, I, 293; II, 129, 157.
13 See Journals of Ralph Waldo Emerson, ed. Edward Waldo Emerson and Waldo Emerson Forbes, 10 vols. (Boston and N.Y., 1909-1914), II, 332-333; JMN, II, 316.
14 The Works of William E. Channing, D.D., ed. George G. Channing, 6 vols. (Boston 1849), III, 221; I, 238. Pommer states that Ellen convinced Emerson of immortality (pp. 28, 50, 68, 76), but Channing's influence was earlier and perhaps more long lasting in certain ways. It is reasonable to suppose that Ellen's death was an important factor in Emerson's leaving his pulpit.
15 YES, p. 103. Harold C. Goddard has stated that Emerson read the Pensées constantly after leaving college: Studies in New England Transcendentalism (N.Y., 1908), p. 66. 16 Channing, III, 223.
17 JMN, II, 388. Moses Maimonides also noted that evil is a negation--the absence of good: "'All evils are negations.' Thus for man death is evil; death is his non-existence. Illness, poverty, and ignorance

are evils for man; all these are privations of properties:" The Guide for the Perplexed, tr. M. Friedländer (London, 1904), p. 266. Emerson was aware of the controversy between the Pharisees, who believed in resurrection from death, redemption, and rewards, and the Sadducees, who opposed such notions because they were not in the original text of the Pentateuch: see JMN, III, 64,77.
18 Between Man and Man, tr. Ronald Gregor Smith and Maurice Friedman (N.Y., 1965), p. 78.
19 "Emerson's 'Compensation' as Argument and as Art," N E Q, XXXVII (Sept., 1964), 304.
20 L, I, 198, 315; JMN, IV, 42, 346; YES, p. 17.
21 JMN, IV, 221. Emerson again refers to this comment by Carlyle, in English Traits (W, V, 18).
22 The Correspondence of Emerson and Carlyle, ed. Joseph Slater (N.Y. and London, 1964), p. 151; JMN, IV, 88. There are also Hegelian overtones in the concept of immortality based upon the eternal Now. See W. T. Stace, The Philosophy of Hegel (N.Y., 1955), p. 514, note.
23 I and Thou, p. 114. See also pp. 12-13, 33, 136.
24 YES, p. 114.
25 "American Transcendentalism's Escape from Phenomenology" in Transcendentalism and Its Legacy, ed. Myron Simon and Thornton H. Parsons (Ann Arbor, 1966), p. 218.
26 Will Herberg, Judaism and Modern Man (N.Y., 1951), p. 127.
27 W, II, 69. The existential belief that during his lifetime, a man is in a perpetual state of becoming and can be defined only after his death is paralleled by Emerson's poem "The Past" (W, IX, 257-258) and by the "Not of spent deeds, but of doing" of "Threnody" (Ibid., p. 158).
28 W, I, 144.
29 YES, p. 111. "The Poet" also treats this theme.
30 The lives of the patriarchs were always an inspiration to Emerson, who lived comfortably with both his tendency to shy away from the cult of personality (whether it was personality of God or of any religious leader) and his tendency to value the immediacy and familiarity of the personal relationship which the individual ancient Hebrew had with his God. See especially JMN, I, 62.
31 I and Thou, p. 106.
32 Martin Buber, Eclipse of God (N.Y., 1952), p. 100.
33 I and Thou, p. 103.
34 Ibid., p. 64.
35 Herberg, p. 40.
36 W, III, 69. See also W, II, 271, and JMN, II, 83; "Author of Mind."
37 W, VIII, 340, 352. See also JMN, IV, 260; VII, 493.
38 See L, I, 199. And in the essay "Experience," Emerson quoted the "law of Adrastia:" "'that every soul which had acquired any truth, should be safe from harm until another period'" (W, III, 87).
39 I and Thou, p. 17.
40 Jonathan Bishop is correct in his analysis of Emerson's statement of bitterness following Waldo's death (Journals, VI, 166). "For it was precisely the power to comprehend, to make something of the charged facts presented to it, that had characterized his own mind at its best:" Emerson on the Soul (Cambridge, Mass., 1964), p. 191. B. Bernard Cohen also perceives the depth of grief in the poem, but maintains that "Threnody" concludes with a reaffirmation of man's spiritual immortality: "'Threnody:' Emerson's Struggle with Grief," Indiana University Folio, XIV (1948), 13-15.
41 Kierkegaard, p. 147.
42 Quoted in David Greene Haskins, Ralph Waldo Emerson, His Maternal Ancestors (Boston, 1887), pp. 130-131.
43 W, III, 58, 75, 55.
44 W, VI, 25, 28, 48.
45 Freedom and Fate (N.Y., 1961), p. 45.
46 I and Thou, pp. 14-15.
47 Ibid., pp. 16-17. See also pp. 23, 25, 27, for echoes of Wordsworth's concept of the child.
48 The Way of Man (N.Y., 1967), p. 41.
49 Kierkegaard, p. 130. See also Kierkegaard's Concluding Unscientific Postscript.

EMERSON ON THE PSYCHIC POTENTIAL

J. RUSSELL REAVER

The lectures Emerson gave on "The Tragic" and "The Comic" in Boston during the winter of 1839-1840 we can see as significant transitions in his creative career. Coming after his preliminary search for relations between the self and not-self in Nature (1836), his intellectual freedom in "The American Scholar" (1837), and his spiritual independence in "The Divinity School Address" (1838), these lectures served primarily as a way for Emerson to clarify the levels of remaining selfhood found in human responses to life as tragic or comic. In this respect, the lectures cleared the ground for him to explore other areas of experience, free from the trap of an ego-centered attitude claiming that life offers only tragic defeat or absurd spectacle.

The essential psychological problem facing Emerson, I believe, was the distracting stimulation of either despair or ridicule since to rest in either creates a static, self-centered satisfaction. To attempt to go beyond the tragic and comic provided a continuing creative means for the human intellect to accomplish its proper work. Especially to the young Emerson at this point, the whole of man's intellectual and psychic capacity had to be freed from the blocks of the tragic and comic to discover more central goals of ethical meaning that may develop an awareness of spiritual objectivity and human unity. Through his analysis of the tragic, Emerson shows how the intellect holds the tragic in equilibrium as a part of the shading of art, while the intellect controls the comic in the coolness of wit. Both of these resolutions maintain a psychic distance from immediate experience and prevent those emotional indulgences typical of many of Emerson's contemporaries whom Mario Praz studied in The Romantic Agony, with their reveling in the beauties of sadness, death, horror, gloomy landscape, satanic eroticism, sadism, fatal women, and varied emotional perversions. By extension, we may also find a way to clarify our twentieth-century perplexities, depending on whether we feel we are living in an "Age of Anxiety" or an "Age of the Absurd." In his lectures, at least, Emerson was making a serious attempt to free himself from the superficial deception of finding ultimate meanings through the ego-centered responses of despair or laughter.

Beside clearing away such confusions, the lectures help bring us close to another quality of Emerson's sort of "romantic idealism." By following his psychological analysis, we realize that he develops his themes in a loosely inductive way from observing experiences of himself and others until, in each lecture, he reaches a climax where we must depend on a faith in human spiritual potentiality to transcend the limits of the tragic or comic. As René Wellek points out conclusively in Confrontations: Studies in the Intellectual and Literary Relations between Germany, England and the United States during the Nineteenth Century (Princeton, 1965), Emerson early distrusted systematic philosophy. He could already write in his Journal when he was only twenty-one: "Metaphysics teach me admirably well what I knew before" (Journals [1824], I, 378-379). German philosophers provided no creative guides for Emerson because, says Wellek: "He was not interested in the processes of their thinking. He was merely interested in their results, which seemed to him a confirmation of a world-view which contradicted and refuted the materialism of the eighteenth century" (Op. cit., 210-211). From examining Emerson's development in "The Tragic" and "The Comic," we can realize more fully his special faith in the creative unconscious, the intuitive depths of mind having moral resources of balance, equanimity, and control, as well as vital predispositions toward harmony and unity. From such deep structures of mind, providing ideal sources of value, Emerson released the full self of man by avoiding the extremes of either "romantic" philosophy constructed by superficial intelligence or "romantic" feelings developed from impulsive drives for emotional display.

To look more closely, then, at Emerson's processes in these crucial lectures, we find he sets out to use his analytical skill on "The Tragic," which preceded "The Comic" in the lecture series on "Human Life." The opening movement of "The Tragic" recognizes the dark side of life, but this admission leads to differentiating between a view that ends in hopeless tragedy and one that reduces tragedy to its proper sphere and recognizes its value. The next movement calls attention to man's resources for dealing with the tragedy that may still remain; and, at last, the dependence on a capacity superseding the tragic vision.

The gloom of the opening movement becomes intense in such metaphors for personal feelings: "As the salt sea covers more than two thirds of the surface of the globe, no sorrow encroaches in man on felicity." In such a mood we may feel completely blocked and defeated so that we are "preparing to lie down in the snow" (Works, Boston, 1903-1904, XII, 405). In fact, the English temperament seems so susceptible to tragic emotion that to such people, Emerson says, "Melancholy cleaves...as closely as to the strings of an AEolian harp." But instead of yielding to despair, Emerson closes this introductory movement with an appeal to our finding values for ourselves in "vice, pain, disease, poverty, insecurity, disunion, fear, and death" (Ibid.).

Emerson moves on to investigate a way of placing in perspective such inevitable defects that defeat our expectations. With examples from classic Greek tragedy, East Indian mythology, Turkish pre-destination, and folk beliefs, Emerson shows that the notion of brute Fate depends on the mind failing to find any logical connection between cause and effect. As a result, all seems illogical whim. Still, Emerson admits, no matter how civilized and subtle our philosophy may be, we will never be able to omit the weakness and imperfection of life in private, personal spheres where individual satisfaction is now and again hindered. Every one of us can enumerate his particular evils and sorrows.

To Emerson, though, such particular defeats, such "definite evils," as he calls them, do not encompass the truly tragic. Rather, the indefinite, unknown, ominous possibility of life produces the terror of total tragedy. Beyond such tragedy, Emerson begins to provide ways of coping with experience. First, he observes the remarkable elasticity of human nature under stress, the durability in a sufferer that to the observer appears unendurable. Once again, Emerson supports his analysis by the force of analogy, a metaphorical method he has of lifting the vision for us by transplanting it to a different reference: "As the frailest glass bell will support a weight of a thousand pounds of water at the bottom of a river or sea, if filled with the same" (Ibid., 411) so the resilient character can withstand odds with a matching strength.

By continuing this characteristic combination of analytical enumeration supported here and there with imaginative comparison, Emerson shows his essential philosophic method: observation of experience intensified by poetic metaphor.

His further development of thought concerning the tragic depends on observing how time helps us forget and how temperament resists pain. Man is not only durable but "wonderfully plastic" in redirecting his efforts and aims whenever necessary. Already Emerson is moving toward that vision of character as strong as fate, which he developed twenty years later in "Fate" and "Power" of Conduct of Life.

Yet, there remains the indefinite evil: Terror. Up to a point, our experience, sophistication, knowledge of specific evils can remove our opinion of what is indefinitely beyond our control in any way. But as long as our emotions are engaged, as long as we tremble before an ultimate unknown, life holds terror, the truly tragic element. Only here can the role of the intellect, as Emerson sees it, enter into man's salvation from total defeat since, in an effort to maintain equilibrium and avoid exaggeration, the intellect can detach and objectify tragic experience. For a time, art can console man by making him a spectator of humanity. Tragic poetry elevates man's understanding and sympathy. Subjective involvement can be relieved. Aesthetic experience, then, provides the transition away from the ego-centered emotion. But even further beyond the value of tragic art with its universal vision of mankind, lies the region that Emerson calls "pure intellect," from which moral meaning arises once the human being realizes that beyond tragedy there still can be creative application of man's will to know and live where "these passionate clouds of sorrow cannot rise" (Ibid., 417). Emerson is not resigning us to tragedy but is using it as a spur to expand our experience.

From the pervasive, unorganized gloom of the opening movement of "The Tragic," we have progressed through the elementary philosophy of brute fate in Greek tragedy or popular superstition to more enlightened traditions of tragedy as being either resisted and used as a counter spur to action or channeled into impersonal art. The final liberation comes from a faith in man's becoming conscious of his moral and intellectual resources remaining to be fulfilled. Although the lecture stops short at this point, Emerson has led us to the threshold of consciousness he will later cross most fully in "Instinct and Inspiration" of his Natural History of Intellect, where he continues his explicit view of man's psychological experience by the action of the creative Will working through Instinct, the elemental unconscious, by which man's percipiencies are combined, directed, and formed for expressing the deep need for potential goodness and truth among men. Tragedy is transcended in Emerson from a humanism consisting of many facets explored throughout his life from Renaissance Platonism to Reformation Christianity, colored with phases of Orientalism. Within the context of the lecture on "The Tragic" particularly, we receive at the climax an assurance of a Concrete Infinite, a dynamic source of affirmative life, recalling to us how often in his implications Emerson can resemble the Quaker tradition from George Fox to Rufus Jones.

The lecture on "The Comic" completed the balance in Emerson's search for creative involvement beyond ordinary limitations. Again the cycle moves from low, obvious levels to high engagement. In the later twentieth century with so much emphasis on the absurd or ironic in drama and fiction, we can especially appreciate Emerson's admission of life as comic.

At the outset of his lecture Emerson focuses, as he had done in "The Tragic," on the extent to which his subject exists in the human condition. Man appears distinguished in this world by his comic sense because no other creature seems to have it. This human response to absurdity depends on our consciousness that allows us to stand back and recognize fractions from wholes. From our rational expectation of continuity and completeness, we receive the jolt of a sudden twist, turn, or break in the line we are conscious

of expecting. The jolt momentarily makes our sense of logic or normalcy disoriented: we appear mad, crazy, absurd, seen in this fracturing that destroys our expected wholeness or fullness. The explosion of laughter shows the release of tension caused by the shock to reason: we are not mad, the world is. And so we snap back to a conscious acceptance of our measure of meaning.

By familiar inductive analysis, Emerson illustrates comic situations: any isolated object (an umbrella, a turnip) with no usefulness; or the disparity between the idea of the human form and a real body; or the clash of opinion between two traveling companions, one a man of the world, one an inexperienced idealist...all bring out the "yawning delinquencies of practice" providing the "radical joke of life" (Works, VIII, 160). To the concerned conscience, such disparities are tragic; to the intellect they are droll. On all levels we can see the cosmic joke, from any external object to complex situations.

But what values does the comic have? To Emerson its chief value becomes its power to furnish a "balance-wheel in our metaphysical structure" (Ibid., 161). This sense of comedy provides "a tie of sympathy with other men, a pledge of sanity, and a protection from those perverse tendencies and gloomy insanities in which fine intellects sometimes lose themselves" (Ibid., 162). Both comedy and tragedy, then, are necessary phases of man's development, making him human by understanding his relationships to others. But the danger lies in using such sensibilities to excess.

Relying on concrete metaphors of experience after his analysis, Emerson achieves a balance of opposites, convincing us that to be too susceptible to laughter is to make ourselves ridiculous; yet to use wit wisely may be a positive means to mask philosophy: a man hearing a joke in solemn company is like "a stout vessel which has just shipped a heavy sea; and though it does not split it, the poor bark is for the moment critically staggered" (Ibid., 162). Or, good wit is "like ice, on which no beauty of form, no majesty of carriage can plead immunity,--they must walk gingerly, according to the laws of ice, or down they must go, dignity and all" (Ibid., 163).

Although Emerson continues to paint funny situations, he implies that the comic is often not appealing. We may laugh but not condone. As Emerson then shows, the most serious efforts are most susceptible to ridicule because any disproportion in them may seem that much more ridiculous by comparison with the intent. Fondest dreams, hardest work, deepest religion may be the butt of a joke when true aspiration or sincere motive is absent: so religious rite without personal involvement is the joke of jokes. Displacement of a part for the whole always produces a joke: we "mistake the wig for the head" (Ibid., 165). In fact, any inflexible formula for spiritual life may easily become ridiculous at times, as Emerson illustrates with the episode of Captain John Smith having the last laugh on a missionary society in London by sending it an Indian to convert after the society complained that American Indians were not becoming at least church-wardens and deacons.

The comic as well as the tragic can be associated with the darkest sides of life. Tragedy allows us to remain in darkness; comedy brings us a shaft of light. Without our conscious rationality, however, creating the comedy, all may sink into tragic defeat. More examples prove Emerson's point: literary criticism is comic when it rests in classifications; language study is ridiculous if it never gets beyond speech exercises to people; political action becomes ironic when no candidate is capable of carrying out a social ideal.

Our Janus-faced life, our tragicomic seesaw persists in tempting us to turn from one extreme to another. "The same scourge," however, "whips the joker and the enjoyer of the joke" (Ibid., 174). Each of us can be punished by his egoistic concerns since, whether tragic or comic, emotional or mental, they are still confined to a partial level of understanding.

Just as he had closed "The Tragic" with the limits of tragedy, Emerson closes "The Comic" with the limits of comedy. There must still be the ability to go beyond the release of conscious reasoning to the dynamic resources of "wisdom and love" (Ibid., 173), which may come into play after life is seen as absurd and laughter has stopped. For his time and ours, Emerson is telling us that the immature romanticist may indulge his ego in tragic or comic subjectivity. The mature romanticist builds beyond them. After ridicule, lies wisdom. After tragedy, love remains.

The Florida State University

EMERSON AND THE WORLD OF DREAM

VIVIAN C. HOPKINS

Dreams are listed in the Introduction to Nature (1836) with other "unexplained" and perhaps "inexplicable" phenomena: language, sleep, madness, beasts, sex. All of these were mysterious, and all were connected with each other. Words were the tools of Emerson's trade, but they were also keys to the ineffable secrets of the universe. Sleep was prized as a condition of health, at the same time that it opened the gates of poetic inspiration.[1] Dreamless sleep offered the most complete rest to the body; but sleep was sometimes resisted, in an effort to recall an exciting dream. With madness Emerson had some experience: through the life-long depression of his brother Bulkely, the manic interludes of his brother Edward, his friends Jones Very and Stewart Newton, and Nancy Barton the insane woman "screaming herself hoarse at the Poor-house across the brook" from his home (J, V, 422-423. Jan. 24, 1840. JMN, VII, 376). Some of these psychic states found their way into his nightmares. Beasts had a special connection with dreams in Emerson's mind, since in the dream man seemed to live most often in the lower consciousness. He like to quote Madame de Staël: "Animals are the dreams of Nature."[2] "I think," he says, "we go to our own dream for a conception of their consciousness. In a dream I have the same instinctive obedience, the same torpidity of the highest power, the same unsurprized assent to the Monstrous as these [Pythagorean] metamorphosed Men exhibit.... One has a kind of compassionate fear lest they should...have a glimpse of their own forlorn condition. What a horrible calamity would be to them one moment's endowment of reason" (J, III, 306-307. JMN, IV, 296-297).[3] "It is strange," he writes, "that all our life is accompanied by Dreams on the one side and by the animals on the other as monuments of our ignorance or hints to set us on the right road of inquiry" (J, III, 553-554. Aug. 5, 1838. JMN, V, 82).

And sex! However understated are Emerson's expressions concerning it, he recognizes it as the élan vital in the plant, animal, and human world. No one can read Ellen Tucker's poems and letters, or the journal entries of Waldo Emerson, without recognizing the flesh as well as the spirit in his first marriage. Reportedly, his second marriage was founded on a Swedenborgian dream of Lydia Jackson's.[3] While it lacked the rapture of the first, it had its satisfactions as well as its tensions, and sex was indeed a factor. Emerson's reading in Swedenborg may well have been his introduction to the realm of demonology, and certainly Swedenborg considered sex the key to celestial as well as spiritual and human love. Not all of Emerson's recorded dreams admit of sexual interpretation; but a number, as we shall see, would have afforded great delight to Sigmund Freud. Nature represented Emerson's declaration of philosophic faith in 1836: man and nature were mean for each other; they complemented and fulfilled each other; today was the great moment of opportunity; the upper and lower worlds could be made to interact productively; the poet would express the beauty he perceived in the flowing of spirit through the universe. In the years that followed his first book, darker shadows--or, worse, gray stretches of torpidity--appeared; the lower world encroached too far on the intellectual realm in the form of panics, mortgages, the Anti-slavery movement, proofreading, lecture preparation, family illness, and importunate house guests. The basic structure of Nature stood firm; but the search went on for that "true theory" which should make explicable those "unexplained" phenomena of the "Introduction." Hence the continued attention to dreams.

In the lecture "Demonology" dreams appear in a different context, listed with "coincidences, animal magnetism, omens, sacred lots," all of which have some relation to the current term, extra-sensory perception. Animal magnetism was a mixed bag, covering Mesmer's use of metallic tractors, hypnotism, and various forms of spiritualism.[5] The tenth and last in the series "Human Life," it was delivered on February 21, 1839, at the Masonic Temple in Boston. Possibly Emerson saved it for the last because of its appeal to young listeners--perhaps not because it was more elevating than "Love" or "Genius," but spicier than "Home," "School," or "Duty". One might compare the thirty-six-year-old Emerson's choice of this subject, especially for his juniors, to an astronomer's effort today to reach intelligent graduate students hipped on astrology, or to an anthropologist's approach to a similar group steeped in witchcraft. The idol of younger scholars since the bold iconoclasm of The Divinity School Address of 1838, Emerson was in a strategic position to examine these "dark" matters and assess them at their worth.

Indeed, the year 1838-1839, when this lecture series was in preparation, was an exciting one for him, with Alcott submitting manuscripts for criticism, Hedge coming down from Maine for meetings of The Club, Thoreau at work on his Journal and frequently dropping in, Caroline Sturgis paying visits, George Ripley planning his community of harmonious souls, schemes afoot for a Transcendental magazine, Sam Ward sending portfolios of art and introducing the beautiful Southern Anna Barker--and Margaret Fuller writing excited, fervid letters. Perhaps the negative side of "Demonology" was directed especially to Margaret's "taste for gems, ciphers, talismans, omens, coincidences, and birthdays." Waldo later noted in the Memoir that she loved the planet Jupiter, thought September her favorable month, found allegory in names (herself a pearl), associated herself with the carbuncle and her friends with other gems and flowers, and experimented (too successfully) with sortes biblicae.[6] Margaret's enthusiasm was so infectious that her friends could be counted to to catch her viruses, whether they were fortune-telling or woman's rights.

The lecture "Demonology" begins with the reason for exploring these hermetic matters: "Every man has usually in a lifetime two or three hints of this kind which are specially impressive to him. They also shed light on our structure."[7] He makes the relevant point that in sleep, each one retreats into a private world of his own: "The witchcraft of sleep divides with truth the empire of our lives. This soft enchantress visits two children lying locked in each other's arms, and carries them asunder by wide spaces of land and sea, and wide intervals of time...."[8] He proceeds, in an eloquent passage, to note the abdication of reason and the creative power shown both in pleasant dreams and in nightmares: "'Tis superfluous to think of the dreams of multitudes, the astonishment remains that one should dream: that we should resign quietly this deifying Reason, and become the theatre of delirious shows, wherein time, space, persons, cities, animals, should dance before us in merry and mad confusion; a delicate creation outdoing the prime and flower of actual nature, antic comedy alternating with horrid pictures. Sometimes the forgotten companions of childhood reappear...or we seem busied for hours and days in strenuous actions for nothings and absurdities, cheated by spectral jokes and waking suddenly with ghastly laughter, to be rebuked by the cold, lonely, silent midnight, and to rake with confusion in memory among the gibbering nonsense to find the motive of this contemptible cachinnation."

The reason abdicated? Actually, no. In a passage of remarkable insight, Emerson explains: "Dreams have a poetic integrity and truth. This limbo and dust-hole of thought is presided over by a certain reason, too. Their extravagance from nature is yet within a higher nature. They seem to us to suggest an abundance and fluency of thought not familiar to the waking experience. They pique us by independence of us, yet we know ourselves in this mad crowd, and owe to dreams a kind of divination and wisdom. My dreams are not me; they are not Nature, or the Not-me; they are both. They have a double consciousness, at once sub- and ob-jective. We call the phantoms that rise, the creation of our fancy, but they act like mutineers, and fire on their commander; showing that every act, every thought, every cause, is bipolar, and in the act is contained the counteraction. If I strike, I am struck; if I chase, I am pursued."[9] Here the creative power of dreams is emphasized. Emerson's recognition of the sub- and ob-jective qualities of the phenomenon resembles Freud's distinction between the id and the ego. Returning to the "me" and "Not-me" of Nature, he sees this "unexplained" experience actually throwing light on the theory of nature, since the two agents of consciousness operate simultaneously in the dream.

This startling and illuminating discovery has a curious relation to a Journal entry made three months later (May 26, 1839) concerning Frederic Henry Hedge's questioning Emerson's faith in the inter-relation between man and Nature: "If, as Hedge thinks, I overlook great facts in stating the absolute laws of the soul; if, as he seems to represent it, the world is not a dualism, is not a bipolar unity, but is two, is Me and It, then is there the alien, the unknown, and all we have believed and charted out of our deep instinctive hope is a pretty dream" (J, V, 206. JMN, VIII, 200). "Dream" in this passage signifies deceptive illusion. Shaken by Hedge's sharply expressed distrust, Emerson expresses here the kind of skeptical mood which he would develop more fully in "Experience" and "Illusions." For example, "Sleep lingers all our lifetime about our eyes, as night hovers all day in the boughs of the fir-tree;" "Dream delivers us to dream, and there is no end to illusion;" "Life wears to me a visionary face. Hardest roughest action is visionary also. It is but a choice between soft and turbulent dreams."[10] Despite such lapses from faith, Emerson was to revert to the "bipolar unity" as a means of understanding man in relation to nature, and to reaffirm the illumination gained from dreams. To return to the lecture "Demonology:" "Wise and sometimes terrible hints shall in them be thrown to the man of a quite unknown intelligence. He shall be startled two or three times in his life by the justice as well as the significance of these phantasmagoria. Once or twice the conscious fetters shall be unlocked, and a freer utterance attained."[11]

Enlightenment, sometimes of a frightening sort, and particularly, knowledge of the self, proceeds from dreams: "We are led by this experience into the high region of Cause, and acquainted with the identity of very unlike-seeming effects. We learn that notions whose turpitude is very differently reputed proceed from one and the same affection. Sleep takes off the costume of circumstance, arms us with terrible freedom, so that every will rushes to a deed. A skillful man reads his dreams for his self-knowledge, yet not the details, but the quality. What part does he play in them, --a cheerful, manly part, or a poor drivelling part? However monstrous and grotesque their apparitions, they have a substantial truth...." Certain points in this passage are especially interesting. He points out the liberation from the restraints of custom, conscience, moral scruples. The freedom is "terrible;" we assume that the deed "rushed to" is violent. One reads for "self-knowledge, yet not the details, but the quality." Compare Freud: "It has been my experience...that every dream treats of oneself. Dreams are absolutely egotistic."[12] "Our doctrine is not based upon the estimates of the obvious dream-content, but relates to the thought-content...the manifest [vs.] the latent dream-content."[13]

Yet Emerson warns against expecting too much of this vaticination: "The fallacy consists in selecting a few insignificant hints when all are inspired with the same sense. As if one should exhaust his astonishment at the economy of his thumb-nail, and overlook the central causal miracle of his being a man." The line of argument here is the same as that directed against Biblical miracles and the Divinity of Christ in The Divinity School Address. In fact, a Journal entry a week before the "Demonology" lecture (Feb. 14, 1839) asserts that demonology--not dreams, in this instance, but "faith in a Genius," "a family Destiny," a ghost--is "the intensation of the individual nature, the extension of this beyond its due bounds and into the domain of the infinite and universal." And he specifically links this with Christianity: "I find traces of this usurpation in very high places, in Christianity, for example. Christianity, as it figures now in the history of ages, intrudes the element of a limited personality into the high place which nothing but spiritual energy can fill" (J, V, 163-164).

Similarly, in the lecture, special censure is meted out to Goethe's concept of the Daimon or guiding spirit of genius (a concept which had previously fascinated Emerson)--but other passages[14] indicate that he sometimes viewed dreams with the same skepticism: "I set down these things as I find them, but however poetic these twilights of thought, I like daylight,[15] and I find somewhat wilful, some play at blindman's-buff, when men as wise as Goethe talk mysteriously of the demonological. The insinuation is that the known eternal laws of morals and matter are sometimes corrupted or evaded by this gypsy principle, which chooses favorites and works in the dark for their behoof; as if the Laws of the Father of the universe were sometimes talked and eluded by a meddlesome Aunt of the universe for her pets." He notes the curious wrenching of perspective in dream: "A dislocation seems to be the foremost trait of dreams. A painful imperfection almost always attends them. The fairest forms, the most noble and excellent persons, are deformed by some pitiful and insane circumstance. The very landscape and scenery in a dream seem not to fit us, but like a coat or cloak of some other person to overlap and encumber the wearer; so is the ground, the road, the house, in dreams, too long or too short, and if it served no other purpose would show us how accurately nature fits man awake."

Especially interesting is his description of déja vu: "In our dreams the same scenes and fancies are many times associated, and that too, it would seem, for years. In sleep one shall travel certain roads in stage-coaches or gigs, which he recognizes as familiar, and has dreamed that ride a dozen times; or shall walk alone in familiar fields and meadows, which road or which meadow in waking hours he never looked upon. This feature of dreams deserves the more attention from its singular resemblance to that obscure yet startling experience which almost every person confesses in daylight, that particular passage of conversation and action have occurred to him in the same order before, whether dreaming or waking; a suspicion that they have been with precisely these persons in precisely this dialogue, at some former hour, they know not when."[16] This peculiar aspect of recollection provides another link between the conscious and subconscious realms. The reverse side of the coin is the difficulty of remembering dreams, which Emerson describes in vigorous metaphorical language: "Dreams are jealous of being remembered; they dissipate instantly and angrily if you try to hold them. When newly awaked from lively dreams, we are so near them, still agitated by them, still in their sphere, --give us one syllable, one feature, one hint, and we should repossess the whole; hours of this strange entertainment would come trooping back to us; but we cannot get our hand on the first link or fibre, and the whole is lost. There is a strange wilfulness in the speed with which it disperses and baffles our grasp." The phenomenon of forgetting still fascinated Emerson as late

as 1870, when he wrote, again with commanding imagery: "The waking from an impressive dream is a curious example of the jealousy of the gods. There is an air as if the sender of the illusion had been heedless for a moment that the Reason had returned to its seat, and was startled into attention. Instantly, there is a rush from some quarter to break up the dream into a chaos of parts, then of particles, then of ether, like smoke dissolving in a wind; it cannot be disintegrated fast enough or fine enough. If you could give the waked watchman the finest fragment, he could reconstruct the whole; for the moment, he is sure he can and will; but his attention is so divided on the disappearing parts, that he cannot grasp the least atomy, and the last fragment or film disappears before he could say, 'I have it'" (J, X, 314. March, 1870).[17]

Emerson gives a new twist in this lecture to the view of the Hebrews, Greeks, and Romans, that dreams can foretell coming events: "A prophetic character in all ages has haunted them. They are the maturation often of opinions not consciously carried out to statements, but whereof we already possessed the elements. Thus, when awake, I know the character of Rupert, but do not think what he may do. In dreams I see him engaged in certain actions which seem preposterous,--out of all fitness. He is hostile, he is cruel, he is frightful, he is a poltroon. It turns out prophecy a year later. But it was already in my mind as character, and the sibyl dreams merely embodied it in fact...."[18]

In this particular statement--the discovery of latent evil in another person, through dream--Emerson shows a belief contrary to that of Freud, who considered dreams illuminating only the character of the dreamer.[19] Yet Emerson's explanation of this phenomenon makes sense, in terms of Freud's theory of suppressed desires, although it involves <u>perception</u> rather than <u>desire</u>. The awareness of Rupert's wickedness existed in his own subconscious but needed the dream to bring it to the surface. As Emerson puts it: "The soul contains in itself the event that shall presently befall it, for the event is only the actualizing of its thoughts. It is no wonder that particular dreams and presentiments should fall out and be prophetic." He concludes with a recognition of value in the occult, especially as a sign of mystery in the universe--but erects some defences against valuing it too highly: "Meantime far be from me the impatience which cannot brook the supernatural, the vast; far be from me the lust of explaining away all which appeals to the imagination, and the great presentiments which haunt us. Willingly I too say, Hail! to the unknown awful powers which transcend the ken of the understanding.... I think the numberless forms in which this superstition has reappeared in every time and every people indicates the inextinguishableness of wonder in man; betrays his conviction that behind all your explanations is a vast and potent and living Nature, inexhaustible and sublime, which you cannot explain. He is sure no book, no man has told him all. He is sure the great Instinct, the circumambient soul which flows into him as into all, and is his life, has not been searched. He is sure that intimate relations subsist between his character and his fortunes, between him and his world; and until he can adequately tell them he will tell them wildly and fabulously. Demonology is the shadow of Theology. [¶] The whole world is an omen and a sign. Why look so wistfully in a corner? Man is the image of God. Why run after a ghost or a dream? The voice of divination resounds everywhere and runs to waste unheard, unregarded, as the mountains echo with the bleatings of cattle."

Emerson gave this lecture again, in the second Harvard course in philosophy, in 1871; it was first printed by J. Elliot Cabot in the collected works of 1883. Erich Fromm has praised it as "one of the most beautiful and concise statements on the superior rational character of our mental process in sleep.... Emerson's statement is significant because he recognizes more clearly than anyone had recognized before him the connection between character and the dream."[20]

Despite his caution against pursuing "a ghost or a dream," Emerson continued, as he had done from 1832 onward, to record his night visions and to seek illumination from them. Some Journal passages underline their significance. For example, in 1833, after seeing Herculaneum and Pompeii, he writes: "Judge of your natural character by what you do in your dreams. If you yield to temptation there, I am afraid you will, awake. If you are a coward there, I jalouse of your courage by day" (J, III, 74. JMN, IV, 71). While the essay "Demonology" shows a recognition similar to Freud's, that the dream cannot be literally interpreted, this passage, by contrast, indicates a simpler, more direct view. Havelock Ellis supports Emerson's statement--at least to the extent that <u>some</u> dreams may be interpreted straight, that is, without reconstruction: "To hold that the Unconscious is always, or even often, in disharmony with the Conscious is a distortion of the facts. He is indeed an unfortunate person whose Unconscious is always out of harmony with his Conscious.... We have only to appeal to dreams which furnish the most familiar revelation of the Unconscious. It must be within the experience of most normal people that dreams perpetually bring

back to us, with even a heightened beauty or tenderness, the facts and emotions of our conscious waking life. Dreams are sometimes a revelation of concealed disharmonies. They are also the most brilliant proof we possess of unsuspected harmonies between our conscious and unconscious lives."[21]

In 1837 Emerson wrote: "Culture inspects our dreams also. The pictures of the night will always bear some proportion to the visions of the day" (JMN, V, 398. Cf. "Spiritual Laws," W, II, 148). This point resembles Freud's idea that something in the preceding day touched off the dream--even though the content might revert to childhood.[22] In "The Over-Soul," dreams are listed with conversation, reveries, remorse, times of passion and surprises, as a means of seeing "ourselves in masquerade, --the droll disguises only magnifying and enhancing a real element and forcing it on our distant notice..." (W, II, 270).

The "double consciousness" explained in "Demonology" is somewhat differently stated in a Journal passage of March, 1848: "In dreams the ordinary theory is that there is but one person; the mystical theory is that there are two or more" (J, VII, 409).[23] This aspect, he suggests, "may explain the magnetic directed dream," i.e., that of a person under hypnosis. In this situation, the hypnotist becomes the creator, and his subject the passive receiver of suggestions; the double consciousness of the dreamer actually becomes two people. It is significant that he remarked this after dreaming of a duel (J, IV, 287. Aug. 21, 1837. JMN, V, 371). Although skeptical of the contemporary craze for hypnotism, he did not consider it an evil practice, as did Browning and Hawthorne--possibly because Lidian refrained from experimenting with it as a cure, while Elizabeth Barrett and Sophia Peabody actually ventured on that dangerous ground.

In September, 1857, he exalts the "truth telling" of dreams over that of table-tipping, and speaks of the creation achieved by them: "I owe real knowledge and even alarming hints to dreams, and wonder to see poeple extracting emptiness from mahogany tables, when there is vaticination in their dreams. For the soul in dreams has a subtle synthetic power which it will not exert under the sharp eyes of day. It does not like to be watched or looked upon, and flies to real twilights, as the rappers do in their wretched mummeries." He describes the dream which occasioned this reflection: When I higgled for my dime and half-dime in the dream, and lost, --the parrots on the chimney tops and church pinnacles scoffed at me, Ho! Ho!" Obviously he is censuring his own desire for gain and judging himself severely: "If in dreams you see loose and luxurious pictures, an inevitable tie drags in the sequel of cruelty and malignity. If you swallow the devil's bait, you will have a horizon full of dragons shortly" (J, IX, 120-121).

In the lecture "Memory," given in the Harvard philosophy courses of 1870-1871, he recognizes the speed of actions in dreams: "The acceleration of mental process is equivalent to the lengthening of life. If a great many thoughts pass through your mind you will believe a long time has elapsed, many hours or days. In dreams a rush of many thoughts, of seeming experiences, of spending hours and going through a great variety of actions and companies, and when we start up and look at the watch, instead of a long night we are surprised to find it a short nap. The opium eater says, 'I sometimes seemed to have lived seventy or a hundred years in one night.' You know what is told of the experience of some persons who have been recovered from drowning. They relate that their whole life's history seemed to pass before them in review" (W, XII, 80).

On January 9, 1832, not quite two years after Ellen's death, he wrote in his Journal: "Hideous dreams last night and queried today whether they were any more than exaggerations of the sins of the day. We see our own evil affections embodied in frightful physiognomies. The account of Flaxman quoted in N. Jerusalem Mag. no. 52 fell in with this.... [The sculptor creates a knight who, falling into the 'nether abyss of sensuality,' is restored to life...only to behold terrific shapes from which he recoils.... A voice whispers, 'Dost thou fear the sight? only thou seest thy inward self--these are thine own fiery and evil passions, who dance and sport in thine imagination, till they have turned thy brain and shipwrecked thy reason" (J, V, 159).] I have read that on the Alps or Andes the traveller sometimes sees a singular phenomenon, his own shadow upon the mist magnified to a giant so that every gesture of his hand is terrific. So it seems to me does every man see himself, in colossal, in the world without knowing that it is himself he sees. The good that he sees compared to the evil that he sees is as his own good to his own evil" (J, II, 448. JMN, III, 317-318. Cf. "Spiritual Laws," W, II, 148). At this time he was still grieving for Ellen, was bored with his Biblical lectures, and beginning to question his fitness for the ministry. Whatever the cause, the content of the dreams is withheld, and the focus turned to explanation and to the parallel in Flaxman's narrative.

By contrast, in Rome at Easter time, overwhelmed by the glory of St. Peter's, he records a pleasant experience: "Rome fashions my dreams. All night I wander amidst statues and fountains, and last night was introduced to Lord Byron!"[24] (J, III, 92. April 13, 1833. JMN, IV, 159).

A slight physical disability (a tic) caused him considerable embarrassment. Because his facial muscles were especially likely to twitch after immoderate laughter, he found Margaret Fuller irritating on first acquaintance--she made him laugh too much. Of "the foolish face of praise" he writes in "Self-reliance:" "The muscles, not spontaneously moved, but moved by a low aspiring wilfulness, grow tight about the outline of the face and make the most disagreeable sensation" (W, II, 55). This idiosyncrasy explains the notation of August 30, 1834: "It is extremely disagreeable, nay, a little fiendish to laugh amid dreams. In bed I would keep my countenance, if you please" (J, III, 334. JMN, IV, 316). Thirty-two years later when this disability was still troubling him, he reiterated "the surprise and curiosity of a stranger or indifferent observer to the trait or the motive and information communicated." This time he dramatized the situation: "Some refractory youth, of whom I had some guidance or authority, expressed very frankly his dissent and dislike, disliked my way of laughing. I was curious to understand the objection, and endeavoured to penetrate and appreciate it, and, of course, with the usual misfortune, that when I woke and attempted to recover the specification, which was remarkable, it was utterly forgotten" (J, X, 174-175. Oct. 24, 1866).

Surely these reports represent self-examination, albeit of a trivial matter. Other dreams probe deeper. For example, "In my dream I saw a man reading in the Library at Cambridge, and one who stood by said, 'He readeth advertisements;' meaning that he read for the market only, and not for truth. Then I said, 'Do I read advertisements?' " (J, V, 356. Dec. 22, 1839. JMN, VII, 327). Emerson's growing success as a lecturer is involved in this dream. Currently engaged in the series, "The Present Age," in Boston, he might well have been suffering a doubt whether lecturing truly meant the enlightenment of his hearers or was only a means of making a living.[25] The fear of failure on the lecture platform occurs in a more elaborate vision twenty-eight years later, when his reputation as an able speaker had extended to the West and to England. He wrote on February 16, 1861: "Last night a pictorial dream fit for Dante. I read a discourse somewhere to an assembly, and rallied in the course of it to find that I had nearly or quite fallen asleep. Then presently I went into what seemed a new house, the inside wall of which had many shelves... on which great and costly vases of Etruscan and other richly adorned pottery stood. The wall itself was unfinished, and I presently noticed great cliffs, intended to be filled with mortar or brickwork, but not yet filled, and the wall which held all these costly vases, threatening to fall. Then I noticed in the centre shelf or alcove of the wall a man asleep, whom I understood to be the architect of the house. I called to my brother William, who was near me, and pointed to this sleeper as the architect, when the man turned, and partly arose, and muttered something about a plot to expose him. When I fairly woke, and considered the picture, and the connection of the dream, --what could I think of the purpose of Jove who sends the dream?" (J, IX, 302-303).

This dream challenges interpretation. Freud's belief that the house represents a sexual symbol does not seem helpful here. But other national and personal concerns do seem relevant. The preceding January 24, he met his first total defeat at a Boston meeting of the Anti-Slavery Society, presided over by Wendell Phillips, when the audience booed him and shouted him down.[26] On April 23, 1861, he delivered his hard-hitting "Civilization at a Pinch" in his Boston course on Literature and Life. Terrible though war was, it seemed to him a necessary scourge for the worse evil of slavery.[27] At the same time, lecture income fell off, because of the universal preoccupation with the war. The great cliffs and the tottering wall in the vision of February, 1861, obviously represented his awareness of the threat to the American republic. The sleeping lecturer probably symbolizes Emerson's doubt of his own powers, and the shift in the sleeper's role, from lecturer to architect, is a familiar dream phenomenon. The friendly interdependence of Waldo and his elder brother William was a lifelong affair, from their early cooperation in schoolkeeping to William's death in 1868, involving financial arrangements, family visits, and intellectual companionship. It was natural for Waldo in distress to look to brother William for help.[28] The "richly adorned pottery" may well be Emerson's own intellectual wares, obscured by the gathering war clouds. The vividness of picture in this dream, a-typical of Emerson's night visions, may indicate the depths from which these doubts were dredged up.

I have found only one dream where Emerson seems to vindicate himself: "Struggled hard last night in a dream to repeat and save a thought or sentence spoken in the dream: but it eluded me at last; only came

out of the pulling, with this rag ,--'His the deeper problem, / But mine the better ciphered' " (J, X, 212. Sept. 1, 1867). A brief but eloquent dream, entered in the Journal on October 24, 1840, reveals a feeling of great power expressed in Miltonic imagery: "I dreamed that I floated at will in the great Ether, and I saw this world floating also not far off, but diminished to the size of an apple. Then an angel took it in his hand and brought it to me and said, 'This must thou eat.' And I ate the world" (J, V, 485).

The first part of this record interests us today because of its similarity to the astronauts' description of the earth as seen from outer space. The second obviously reveals the trait of egotism, a characteristic for which many people (including Lidian Emerson) reproached Waldo.[29] Moreover, Freud's discovery of sexual significance in "flying" dreams has relevance. The correspondence with Caroline Sturgis and Margaret Fuller has already been mentioned; that with Margaret was especially frequent during the Dial years, 1840-1844. Four days before this entry (October 20, 1840), Waldo wrote Margaret an excited letter: "A strong passion, or the opportunity of a great work accurately adapted to one's latent faculties, --these are the sudden schoolmasters.... Nothing less than such as these could give me a look through your telescope or you one through mine;--an all explaining look. Let us float along through the great heavens a while longer [italics mine] and whenever we come to a point whence our observations agree, the time when they did not will seem but a moment... (L, II, 349). I have not seen Margaret's reply, but it must have exceeded Waldo's in enthusiasm. On October 24, the same day that he recorded this dream, he replied, warding her off: "I have your frank and noble and affecting letter, and yet I think I could wish it unwritten.... There is a difference in our constitution. We use a different rhetoric.... Speak to me of every thing but myself and I will endeavor to make an intelligent reply..." (L, II, 352-353).[30] Read in Miltonic terms, the dream means giving in to temptation. Was it a warning to resist whatever Margaret was offering? Emerson's terror may well be reflected in the next Journal entry, October 26, a vision of Guy-Theanor concerning murder and disease, not labeled a dream, but with all the qualities of a nightmare (JMN, VII, 525). Scarcely a month later (November 21, 1840), he described another dream, with more obvious sexual symbolism: "A droll dream last night, whereat I ghastly laughed.[31] A congregation assembled, like some of our late conventions, to debate the institution of marriage; and grave and alarming objections stated on all hands to the usage; when one speaker at last rose and began to reply to the arguments, but suddenly extended his hand and turned on the audience the spout of an engine which was copiously supplied from within the wall with water, and whisking it vigorously about, up, down, right and left, he drove all the company in crowds hither and thither and out of the house. Whilst I stood watching, astonished and amused at the malice and vigor of the orator, I saw the spout lengthened by a supply of hose behind, and the man suddenly brought it round a corner and drenched me as I gazed. I woke up relieved to find myself quite dry, and well convinced that the institution of marriage was safe for tonight" (J, V, 499. JMN, VII, 544).

A Freudian would discount Emerson's pat interpretation of this dream. But again, from the analyst's point of view, circumstances immediately preceding this entry show that he had cause for anxiety concerning his married life. Apart from the importunities of Cary Sturgis and Margaret Fuller, there was a threat from the new community which George Ripley was proposing. Lidian went to visit her brother in Boston early in November and stayed longer than she had planned. Waldo wrote to her on November 15, jocosely urging her not to set sail on the Britannia: "The 'Community' question is in full agitation betwixt Mr. Ripley Mr. Alcott and me and if you wish to have a voice in it and not to find your house sold over your head or perhaps a troop of new tenants brought suddenly into it you must come and counsel your dangerous husband.... You must love your husband all you can" (L, II, 360-361).

Brook Farm community did indeed threaten the institution of marriage, especially in the later years when Fourierism entered the picture; Almira Barlow cast sheep's eyes at the men; the school children had a co-educational dormitory;--and so on. Emerson's decision not to join was chiefly economic, because of his investment in the Concord house; but he may well have seen this venture as a possible disrupter of domestic tranquillity.[32]

In March, 1842, he reflected that nightmare could teach the emotion of terror which man might not otherwise experience: "Neither public nor private violence, neither natural catastrophes, as earthquake, volcano, or deluge; nor the expectation of supernatural agents in the form of ghosts, or of purgatory and devils and hell fire, disturb the sleeping circulations of the blood in these calm, well-spoken days. And yet dreams acquaint us with what the day omits." He then recorded the dream which occasioned this conclusion: "I found myself in a garret disturbed by the noise of some one sawing wood. On walking towards

the sound, I saw lying in a crib an insane person [Bulkely?] whom I very well knew, and the noise instantly stopped; there was no saw, a mere stirring among several trumpery matters, fur muffs and empty baskets that lay on the floor. As I tried to approach, the muffs swelled themselves a little, as with wind, and whirled off into a corner of the garret, as if alive, and a kind of animation appeared in all the objects in that corner. Seeing this, and instantly aware that here was Witchcraft, that here was a devilish Will which signified itself plainly enough in the stir and sound of the wind, I was unable to move; my limbs were frozen with fear; I was bold and would go forward, but my limbs I could not move; I mowed the defiance I could not articulate, and woke with the ugly sound I made" (J, VI, 178-180. March, 1842).

The same sense of helplessness characterizes a particularly gruesome nightmare which Emerson experienced in Paris in May, 1848, when, as seems likely, the external events of the brief revolution, rather than internal pressures, were responsible. He wrote a vivid account concerning the stirring events of the fifteenth to his wife on May 17. The dream was recorded previously, but when arming was in progress: "What games sleep plays with us! We wake indignant that we have been so played upon, and should have lent ourselves to such mountains of nonsense. All night I was scarifying with my wrath some conjuring miscreant, but unhappily I had an old age in my toothless gums, I was as old as Priam, could not articulate, and the edge of all my taunts and sarcasms, it is to be feared, was quite lost. Yet, spite of my dumb palsy, I defied and reared after him, and rattled in my throat, till wife waked me up. Then I bit my lips. So one day we shall wake up from this longer confusion, and be not less mortified that we had lent ourselves to such rigmarole" (J, VII, 458). Emerson's conclusion, that release from life would offer a deliverance similar to that of waking from a bad dream, does not seem particularly satisfying. But the dream itself is powerfully described and may well indicate that the revolution frightened him more than he liked to admit. How it contrasts with the laconic daytime entry: "The scholar was glad to leave his manuscript and go to the window!" (J, VII, 460).

Aside from the reference to Rupert's rascality in "Demonology" Emerson recorded no prophetic dream of his own. But he did have a premonition of Webster's death. At Plymouth, New Hampshire, Oct. 24, 1852, he was "looking across the hazy water toward Marshfield and thinking that Webster must have died. Webster had died at three o'clock that morning."[33] The circumstances here are interesting. Webster's illness was known; the nearness to his environs brought him keenly to mind; Emerson had castigated him severely in his address "The Fugitive Slave Law" and in the "Ode to Channing" because Webster had supported the "odious" law. Immediately after the Senator's death, Emerson recalled his former greatness and began to regret his share in the attacks by Northern liberals.

In a lighter connection, Emerson was amused by a more trivial prophetic dream: "Mr. Charles P. Ware tells Edward that the night before the Commemoration Day he spent at Mr. Hudson's room, in Cambridge, and woke from a dream which he could not remember, repeating these words, --'And what they dare to dream of, dare to die for.' He went to the Pavilion Dinner, and there heard Mr. Lowell read his poem, and when he came to the lines: 'These love her best who to themselves are true / And what --' Ware said, 'Now I know what's coming--but it won't rhyme;' and Mr. Lowell proceeded, --'they dare to dream of, dare to do' " (J, X, 309-310. Feb. 3, 1870).

Several dreams were philosophical. On January 3, 1837, following an analysis of the "mysterious and delightful surprise" involved in aesthetic experience, he wrote: "After I got into bed, somewhat else rolled through my head and returned betwixt dreams,[34] which I fear I have lost. It seems as if it were to this purport: that every particular composition takes its fit place in the intellectual sphere; the light and gay, a light and fugitive place; the wise, a permanent place; but only those works are everlasting which have caught, not the ephemeral and local, but the universal symbols of thought, and so written themselves in a language that needs no translation into the sympathies and intellectual habits of all men. Homer and Shakespear" (J, IV, 180. Jan. 3, 1837. JMN, V, 278-279). This observation is arresting, showing an interweaving of the conscious and semi-conscious states occurring "betwixt dreams"--imperfectly remembered and yet making a significant point about the ranking of literary works.

Two remarkable visions, recorded in 1841, carry on the theme of "The Over-Soul," which was published in Essays, First Series, January 1, 1841. Both experiences involve a persona--like the idealized Guy and Osman of some Journal passages, or the Uriel and Seyd (or Saadi) of the poems. The first, described April 24, 1841, involves an element of terror which suggests the sublime: "I beheld him and he

turned his eyes on me, his great serious eyes. Then a current of spiritual power ran through me, and I looked farther and wider than I was wont, and the visages of all men altered and the semblance of things. The men seemed to me as mountains, and their faces seamed with thought, and great gulfs between them, and their tops reached high into the air. And when I came out of his sight, it seemed to me as if his eyes were a great river, like the Ohio, or the Danube, which was always pouring a torrent of strong, sad light on some men wherever he went, and tingeing them with the quality of his soul" (J, V, 537. JMN, VII, 439). The second, more extensively developed, is recorded in early May, 1841: "I walked in my dream with a pundit who said...he could not speak with me many words, for the life of incarnate natures was short, but that the vice of men was old age, which they ought never to know; for, though they should see ten centuries, yet would they be younger than the waters, which--hearken unto their sound! how young is it, yet how old!" The dream expresses the concepts of surmounting the sorrows of this world by "living in the All;" of the deities of various civilizations--Jove, Apollo, Osiris, Vishnu, Odin, Christ--as "coins of different countries" to represent the Over-Soul; and of necessary interaction between man's spirit and that of the universe. The single "external fact" considered here is that of hospitality. Emerson's attitude toward this was indeed bi-polar; he was constantly inviting people to the house--and a goodly number came uninvited--for meals and lodging; yet he constantly bewailed in his Journal the time lost to visitors. The "pundit" may well be recommending the virtue of hospitality to an unwilling self: "The troops of guests who succeed each other as inmates of our houses and messmates at our tables, week after week, are recording angels who inspect and report our domestic behavior, our temperance, our conversation and manners; therefore, the pure in heart having nothing to hide, are the most hospitable, or keep always open house. But to those who have something to conceal, every guest is unwelcome" (J, V, 550-551. JMN, VII, 449).[35]

Freud's theory does not offer much light on this kind of dream, since his discussion of "ideas" in dreams involves only simple concepts.[36] But these "Over-soul" dreams--the terror and power of the first and the haunting poetry of the second--do illustrate Jung's theory of the "collective unconscious." Consider how Jung describes his "subjective view of the world:" "A vision such as will come to one who undertakes, deliberately, with half-closed eyes and somewhat closed ears, to see and hear the form and voice of being."[37] Erich Fromm's view is also pertinent: "My assumption is that dreams can be the expression both of the lowest and most irrational _and_ of the highest and most valuable functions of our minds."[38]

Another reflective dream, twenty-eight years later, is less fully recorded: "I wish I could recall my singular dream of last night with its physics, metaphysics, and rapid transformations--all impressive at the moment, that on waking at midnight I tried to rehearse them, that I might keep them till morn. I fear 'tis all vanished. I noted how we magnify the inner world, and emphasize it to hypocrisy by contempt of house and land and man's condition, which we call shabby and beastly. But in a few minutes these have their revenge, for we look to their chemistry and perceive that they are miracles of combination and ethereal elements and do point instantly to moral causes" (J, X, 301-302. Oct. 21, 1869).[39] Again, the message seems a warning to the philosopher from his subconscious, not to scorn material things.

Of seventeen dreams recorded between 1832 and 1867, six are grim (Jan. 9, 1832; Aug. 30, 1834; March, 1842; May, 1848; Feb. 16, 1861; Oct. 24, 1855); two, grotesque (Nov. 21, 1840; Sept., 1857); one self-critical, in a dispassionate mood (Dec. 22, 1839); one self-vindicating (Sept. 1, 1867); one expressing temptation and a sense of power (Oct. 24, 1840); five philosophical (Jan. 3, 1837; Aug. 15, 1838; Jan. 1, early May, 1841; Oct. 21, 1869); and only one entirely pleasant (April 13, 1833). Self-criticism is also involved in several of the grim and philosophical dreams. An over-view of Emerson's essays, poems, letters, and journals shows that negative moods, however vividly expressed, are occasional rather than habitual; they are the reverse side of a dominantly bright tapestry; the Under-soul of the Over-Soul; the minor transition key which throws into relief the major key--optimistic, hopeful, hortatory.[40] The opposite seems true of Emerson's subconscious life, where the grim, grotesque, unpleasant visions (what he calls "turbulent" dreams) dominate over the "soft" or satisfying. One might hypothesize that a special function of dreams for this writer was katharsis. Quite possibly these night visions, and his reflections on them, helped him to maintain equilibrium in a shifting world.

The philosophical dreams are another matter. As we have seen, they present a most interesting aspect of the subconscious, not at all illuminated by the psychology of Freud, and only partially by that of Jung. Developing further the thoughts of the day, in flashes of insight they show a relationship to such visions as Coleridge's opium dream of _Kubla Khan_ and to the scientist Otto Loewi's discovering in a dream

the chemical theory of transmitting nervous impulses.41 The Neo-Platonic tradition, so significant in Emerson's thought, also has relevance here--the concept that inspiration comes more readily to the sleeping spirit freed from the domination of the senses.42 While Emerson does not specify either Plato or Plotinus as a frame of reference for his dreams, he clearly has the Neo-Platonic theory in mind when he says: "The oldest and most deserving person should come very modestly into any newly awaked company, respecting the divine communications out of which all must be presumed to have newly come" ("Behaviour," VI, 196-197). Not only the "floating dream" of October 24, 1840, but all the philosophical dreams have some affinity with the "magic flight" of ancient religions, described by Mircea Eliade: "The 'flight' signifies intelligence, the understanding of secret things and metaphysical truths.... There remain always the two essential motifs...transcendence and freedom, both the one and the other obtained by a rupture of the plane of experience, and expressive of an ontological mutation of the human being."43

Emerson recorded not only his own dreams, but also those of others. For example: "There are parts of your nature deep and mysterious. I knew a man who stabbed the name and character of another; and at night he saw a murderer's face grinning and gibbering over him" (JMN, V, 113. Jan. 16, 1836). He copied from Alcott's manuscripts notes about the dreams of his daughter (Anna or Louisa): "Her dreams are so vivid and impressive that they are taken for realities of sense, and she refers to them afterwards as facts in her experience. So strong is her faith in them, that no reasoning, not even the faith she places in the assurance of her parents, makes her relinquish the conviction. [¶] Thus unconsciously, even to us perchance, doth our waking and sleeping life coalesce and lose their separate forms in one predominating sentiment or idea, and take a common unity in the spirit from whence they sprung into life and shaping" (J, IV, 11, 1836). Alcott's interpretation of the dream world is simpler than Emerson's, but similar in recognizing the uniting of the two worlds by means of their spiritual origin.

A "recurring" dream of Margaret Fuller is noted: "The same dream recurs to her periodically, annually, and punctually to its night. The dream she marks in her journal is repeated for the fourth time: 'In C.[aroline Sturgis], I at last distinctly recognized the figure of the early vision, whom I found after I had left A., who led me on the bridge, towards the city, glittering in the sunset, but mid way, the bridge went under water. I have often seen in her face that it was she, but refused to believe it.'"44 The colorful sky and water imagery admirably reveal the hectic friendship between Margaret and the younger Caroline: Caroline's admiration, tempered by wilfulness; Margaret's direction of Cary's reading and social life; and Margaret's feeling that they were indeed soulmates.

Particularly arresting is the dream of Lidian Emerson, recorded November 18, 1841, four days before Edith's birth: "Queenie's dream of the statue so beautiful that the blooming child who was in the room looked pale and sallow beside it, and of the speech of the statue, which was not quite speech either, but something better, which seemed to the fair girl who sat by, and whose face became flushed with her earnest attention--life and being;--and then, by a few slight movements of the head and body, it gave the most forcible picture of decay and death and corruption, and then became all radiant again with the signs of resurrection" (J, VI, 129-130. Nov. 18, 1841). Herein Lidian rivals her husband in imaginative creation. Curiously, instead of considering this the apprehensive fantasy of a woman in the final stage of pregnancy, Emerson makes a literary interpretation: "I thought it a just description of that Eloquence to which we are all entitled--are we not?--which shall be no idle tale, but the suffering of the action, and action it describes." From the Brihaa Arangaka Upanishad Emerson copied a charming description of the dreamer's creative power: "When he sleeps, then becomes this Purusha [spirit] unmingled light. No chariots are there, no horses, no roads; then he creates chariots, horses, roads; no pleasures are there, no tanks, no lakes, no rivers; then he creates joys, tanks, lakes, rivers; for he is the agent" (J, IX, 302-303).

Dreams helped Emerson understand himself, other persons, and the natural world. They also illuminate his view of the creative imagination. "The I partial makes the dream," he explains; "the I total, the interpretation" (Ms. Lecture, "Demonology"). What the ordinary man knows of the creative process, he suggests, is derived largely from dreams, during which he gets the "feel" of the creative consciousness, at the same time as he remains an observer. The dream is a key to the secret of creation in the plastic arts: "We may owe to dreams some light on the fountain of this skill; for as soon as we let our will go and let the unconscious states ensue, see what cunning draughtsmen we are! We entertain ourselves with wonderful forms of men, of women, of animals, of gardens, of woods and of monsters, and the mystic pencil wherewith we then draw has no awkwardness or inexperience, no meagreness or poverty; it can design well

and group well; its composition is full of art, its colors are well laid on and the whole canvas which it paints is lifelike and apt to touch us with terror, with tenderness, with desire and with grief" ("Intellect," W, II, 337-338. Cf. JMN, VII, 141, 143).

Just as dreams revealed the dark places in his own subconscious, that "Chimborazo under the line" of the waking mind, so did they explain the terrible in literature. In such widely differing creators as Blake, Michelangelo, Shakespeare (in Macbeth and Lear), Milton, Aeschylus, and Dante, he found the terrible vividly expressed. He sought to define it: "Is the dire the act of the imagination when groping for its symbols in these parts or functions of nature which nature conceals because painful to the observer?" (Ms. Lecture, "Demonology"). In this view, the creative artist is conceived as drawing up from the subconscious those frightening images which are suppressed in the ordinary course of life. From the terror of dreams, the average man is enabled to comprehend that element in literature or art. In fact, the dream itself, and its recollection, may become an aesthetic experience. Of his nightmare of March, 1842, Emerson says: "After I woke and recalled the impressions, my brain tingled with repeated vibrations of terror; and yet was the sensation pleasing, as it was a sort of rehearsal of a Tragedy" (J, VI, 180).

By contrast, a Journal criticism uses the dream as a means of denigrating Dante, placing him below Shakespeare, Socrates, and Goethe: "Dante still appears to me, as ever, an exceptional mind, a prodigy of imaginative function, executive rather than contemplative or wise. Undeniable force of a peculiar kind, a prodigy, but not like Shakespeare, or Socrates, or Goethe, a beneficent humanity.... The somnambulic genius of Dante's dream strengthened to the tenth power, --dream so fierce that it grasps all the details of the phantom spectacle, and, in spite of itself, clutches and conveys them into the waking memory, and can recite what every other would forget.... Abnormal throughout like Swedenborg" (J, X, 210. 1867). This judgment had been preceded by a long and devoted study of Dante, including a translation of the Vita Nuova. One must of course remember that Shakespeare, Socrates, and Goethe were also removed from their pedestals, when measured by the lofty transcendental aesthetic. And the dream imagery here does convey a sense of the hectic, feverish quality in the Inferno and Purgatorio--"fierce," "abnormal," "somnambulic genius."

Emerson had no Dream-Book by which to interpret his night visions. Two works dealing with the occult are mentioned in "Demonology:" Walter Scott, Lectures on Demonology and Witchcraft (London, 1830) and the Report of the Experiments on Animal Magnetism...by a Committee...of the French Royal Academy of Sciences, tr. J. C. Colquhoun (Edinburgh, 1833). Scott's work is directed chiefly toward ghosts and demons. The only hint concerning dreams which Emerson may have taken from it is his statement about dual personality.[45] The French report, devoted to Mesmer's experiments, does not consider dreams. The "bewildering," "besmirching" effect of these two books is contrasted with the writings of two philosophers: "Read a page of Cudworth or of Bacon, and we are exhilarated and armed to manly duties." Of these, Cudworth offered something very pertinent to Emerson's view of double consciousness when he speaks of "another more interior kind of plastic power in the soul." "Whereby it is formative of its own cogitations, which itself is not always conscious of; as when, in sleep or dreams, it frames interlocutory discourses betwixt itself and other persons, in a long series, with coherent sense and apt connexions, in which oftentimes it seems to be surprised with unexpected answers and repartees, though itself were all the while the poet and inventor of the whole fable."[46]

Erich Fromm mentions Goethe's statement in Conversations with Eckermann concerning the heightened activity of the mind during sleep.[47] Although Emerson read this work carefully, in Margaret Fuller's translation (Boston, 1839), this particular point does not seem to have impressed him. "Wise old Plutarch" was Emerson's authority for distrusting all demonological phenomena--[48] but there were depths in his own subconscious experience not encompassed by Plutarchian common sense. Clearly Emerson's careful recording of his night visions, as well as the content of his dreams, anticipates some present-day psychological theories and methods. Even though his explanations of dreams are often less satisfactory than his descriptions, this whole realm reveals a developing self-knowledge. I find William E. Bridges' relating Emerson's thought to contemporary parapsychology quite persuasive;[49] Erich Fromm's admiration for Emerson's "Demonology" is an added link in this chain of evidence. I believe, however, that some aspects of Emerson's dream material show an affinity also to Freud and Jung--but by no means all. Could we imagine Emerson perusing Freud today, we should probably find him agreeing with Jung and Ellis, that Freud was too narrow in referring all dreams to some sexual trauma or wish-fulfillment. Doubtless, too, he would censure Freud's

rigid interpretations of certain objects: for example, the house, the tower, the water-spout, in the same way he criticized Swedenborg's limitation of the horse, the tree, the moon, to a single rather than a multiple symbolic meaning. Emerson makes no such distinction between "false" and "true" dreams as Vergil does with his two gates of ivory and horn. No doubt he considered some more significant than others. He probably jests when he comments on the nightmare of February 16, 1861: "When I fairly woke, and considered the picture, and the connection of the dream, --what could I think of the purpose of Jove who sends the dream?" Or it may be that this passage indicates a sense of connection here with--one might say--a direct line to the Over- or the Under-soul. A perceptive Journal statement concerns the ineffableness of the Divine Being: "There is an important équivoque in our use of the word unconscious, a word which is much played upon in the psychology of the present day. We say that our virtue and genius are unconscious, that they are the influx of God, and the like. The objecter replies that to represent the Divine Being as an unconscious somewhat is abhorrent, etc. But the unconsciousness we spake of was merely relative to us; we speak, we act, from we know not what higher principle, and we describe its circumambient quality by confessing the subjection of our perception to it, we cannot overtop, oversee it, --not see at all its channel into us. But in saying this, we predicate nothing of its consciousness or unconsciousness in relation to itself. We see at once that we have no language subtle enough for distinctions in that inaccessible region" (J, V, 384-385. April 27, 1840. JMN, VII, 344). Unknowable? Yes. But hints on which to build a philosophy have come from outer nature--language, animals, friends of both sexes, the sane as well as the insane--and among these, an important source of depth consciousness is the world of dream.

State University of New York at Albany

---

1 "Sleep for five minutes seems an indispensable cordial to the human system. No rest is like the rest of sleep. All other balm differs from the balm of sleep as mechanical mixture differs from chemical. For this is the abdication of will and the accepting of a supernatural aid" (Journals, ed. Edward Emerson and Waldo E. Forbes, 10 vols. [Boston, 1909-1914], IV, 142-143, Nov. 7, 1836. This edition is hereinafter referred to as "J". The Journals and Miscellaneous Notebooks, ed. William H. Gilman, Alfred R. Ferguson, Merrell R. Davis, Merton M. Sealts, Harrison Hayford, George P. Clark, Ralph H. Orth, A. W. Plumstead (7 vols. covering 1819-1842) [Cambridge, 1960-1969], VI, 241. This scholarly edition hereinafter referred to as "JMN." "Adjourned the promised lecture on Genius until Wednesday week, on account of my unaccountable vigils now for four or five nights, which destroy all power of concentration by day" (J, V, 160. Jan. 1, 1839).

2 Anna de Staël, Germany, 3 vols. in 2 (N.Y., 1814), II, 322. Cf. Plato, Republic, Bk. IX, 572, tr. B. Jewett, 2 vols. (N.Y., 1937), I, 829-830.

3 Cf. "Demonology," The Complete Works (Centenary ed.) 12 vols. (Boston, 1903-1904), X, 11. This edition hereinafter cited as "W." Cf. "Dreams and beasts are two keys by which we are to find out the secrets of our own nature. All mystics use them. They are like comparative anatomy. They are test objects" (J, II, 453. Jan. 21, 1832; JMN, III, 321). Contrast Swift, who endowed the Houhynhnms, if not with reason, at least with superior horse sense. Contrast Whitman's wish to live with "placid and self-contain'd animals: 'They do not sweat and whine about their condition, / They do not lie awake in the dark and weep for their sins, / They do not make me sick discussing their duty to God'" (Song of Myself, Stanza 32).

4 Ralph L. Rusk, Life of Ralph Waldo Emerson (N.Y., 1949), pp. 210-211.

5 For contemporary writings on this subject, especially hypnotism, see Doris V. Falk, "Poe and the Power of Animal Magnetism," PLMA, LXXXIV (May, 1969) 536-546.

6 Emerson, "Concord," Memoirs of Margaret Fuller Ossoli, 2 vols. (Boston, 1852), I, 219-221. If Emerson hoped by means of this lecture to deflect Margaret and her friends from their "magnetic" course, he was not successful. On October 18, 1840, he replied to an enthusiastic letter of Caroline Sturgis: "I am a slow scholar at magnetism, dear sister, and always read the newspaper whilst that subject is discussed.... I must even leave you and Margaret to your flights in the sky, wishing you pleasant airs and a safe alighting" (Letters, ed. Ralph L. Rusk, 6 vols. [N.Y., 1939], II, 346). This edition hereinafter cited as "L." Cf. "To Margaret Fuller, Oct. ?22 ?1840," L, II, 351, expressing gratitude for the love he received at about the same time from "four persons"--Margaret, Sam Ward, Anna Barker, and Caroline Sturgis. Sam and Anna had been married October 3, 1840; Margaret was chagrined, but recovered, and remained a good friend to both. Emerson's essay "Friendship" strongly influenced by these relationships, was finished June 22, 1840.

7 "Demonology," W, X, 9-32.

8 Cf. his quotation from Heraclitus' "Of Superstition" in Plutarch: "There is one world common to all who are awake, but of sleepers, each one betakes himself to a peculiar world of his own" (Morals, 5 vols. [London, 1718], I, 165; JMN, VI, 379). Cf. William James: "When Paul and Peter wake up in the same bed, and recognize that they have been asleep, each one of them mentally reaches back and makes connection with but one of the two streams of thought which were broken by the sleeping hours" (Psychology: Briefer Course [N.Y., 1920], p. 158).
9 This is a reworking of a Journal passage, April 20, 1838, written after a night of "ill dreams:" "Dreams are true to nature, and, like monstrous formations (e.g., the hose-hoof divided into toes) show the law.... If I push, I am resisted" (J, IV, 424. JMN, V, 475). Cf. J, III, 463, March 31, 1835, and JMN, V, 27: "The dreams of an idealist [R. W. E.] have a poetic integrity and truth." Cf. "Brahma:" "I am the doubter and the doubt."
10 "Experience," Essays, Second Series, W, III, 50, 53, 84.
11 Cf. Ms. Lecture "Demonology:" "The text of life is accompanied by the gloss or commentary of dreams."
12 Sigmund Freud, The Interpretation of Dreams, tr. A. A. Brill (N.Y., 1933), p. 308.
13 Ibid., p. 141. Consider also Freud's extensive use of dreams in treating the mentally ill. Emerson illustrates the surfacing of suppressed desires in dreams by the experience of a friend who was a gentleman by day but always a servile drudge in his dreams. He concludes, in language that Freud might have used: "Civil war in our atoms, mutiny of the sub-daemons not yet subdued" (Ms. J. RS, 1848).
14 E.g., "The existing world is not a dream, and cannot with impunity be treated as a dream...." ("The Conservative," W, I, 286). "These hints, dropped as it were from sleep and night, let us use in broad day" ("History," W, II, 7).
15 Cf. the comment on Plutarch: "He believes in witchcraft and the evil eye, in demons and ghosts,--but prefers, if you please, to talk of these in the morning" ("Plutarch," W, VIII, 284). And see Plutarch's own statement: "The Paths of life are large, but in few are men directed by the Daemons" ("Discourse Concerning the Daemon of Socrates," Morals, 2 vols. [Boston, 1870], II, 399; JMN, VI, 74-85). It is interesting to note that Carl Jung uses this Goethean concept to express censure of Freud's referral of all neuroses to sexual trauma: "I see him as a tragic figure; for he was a great man, and what is more, a man in the grip of his daimon" (Memories, Dreams, Reflections [N.Y., 1963], p. 153).
16 It is unlikely that Emerson would accept Freud's explanation of déja vu: "The locality is always the genitals of the mother...." (Interpretation of Dreams, p. 375).
17 Among the reasons for forgetting dreams, Freud lists the weakness of some dream images, the difference between the psychic state of the dream and the conscious state, the force of the "inrushing world of sensation" attacking the dream images, and the fact that most people take little interest in their dreams (Interpretation of Dreams, pp. 57-61). Of these, the second and third points would seem particularly applicable to Emerson's dream world.
18 Note that the comparable Journal passage, reworked for the lecture, does not mention the wickedness uncovered by the dream: "Awake I know the character of Andrew, but do not think what he may do. In dream I turn that knowledge into a fact; and it proves a prophecy" (J, IV, 287. Aug. 21, 1837; JMN, V, 371). The last sentence of the Journal entry indicates that Emerson had been talking the matter over with Hedge: "Why then should not symptoms, auguries, forebodings also be, and, as Hedge said, 'the meanings of the spirit' [?]"
19 Freud, Interpretations of Dreams, pp. 112-114, 308.
20 Erich Fromm, The Forgotten Language: An Introduction to the Understanding of Dreams, Fairy Tales and Myths (N.Y., 1951), pp. 140-142.
22 Freud, Interpretations of Dreams, p. 176.
23 In this passage the "two" confirms the idea of the dreamer as both creator and observer; the "or more" I confess seems inexplicable.
24 Editors Emerson and Forbes suggest that this means he "first rightly appreciated Childe Harold." It seems more likely that Waldo means exactly what he says. He was, of course, reading Byron, and much enjoyed seeing his apartments in Florence (J, III, 108-109. May 2, 1833; JMN, IV, 169).
25 Cf. entry of Sept., 1857, above.
26 Rusk, Life, pp. 408-409.
27 See, e.g., "To James Elliot Cabot, Aug. 4, 1861," L, V, 251-254.
28 Curiously, in the spring and summer of 1861--the period following this dream--William seemed more than usually dependent on Waldo, who was helping William's son Charles out of a scrape at Harvard and doctoring a lame horse that William had left in Concord (L, V, 244-252).
29 Cf. the extract which Waldo notes from his brother Charles's Journal: "Put me by the world-wheels, and if I wouldn't give them a twirl!" (J, IV, 141).
30 Apparently Margaret took the rebuke in good part, since her letter of November 7 shows affection and appreciation of his work (L, II, 354).
31 Cf. entries of Aug. 39, 1834, and Oct. 24, 1866.

32 Emerson's letter to Ripley, December 15, 1840, stating his reasons for not joining, shows that serious--even tormented--self-examination preceded the refusal (L, II, 368-371). 33 Rusk, Life, p. 368.

34 Cf. Poe's more extensive analysis of the ecstasy he enjoyed through "physical impressions" as opposed to thoughts: "They arise in the soul...only at its epochs of most intense tranquillity--when the bodily and mental health are in perfection--and at those mere points of time where the confines of the waking world blend with those of the world of dreams. I am aware of these 'fancies' only when I am upon the very brink of sleep, with the consciousness that I am so" (Marginalia, Complete Works, ed. James A. Harrison, 17 vols. [N.Y., 1902], XVI, 88-89).

35 Cf. a letter to Margaret Fuller, May 6, 1841, talking of his hypochondria and urging her to visit at Concord. The letter uses astronomical imagery to express an idea also found in the dream--expanding time and space to compensate for earthly limitations: "Come, o my friend, with your earliest convenience, I pray you, and let us seize the void betwixt two atoms of air, the vacation between two moments of time to decide how we will steer on the torrent which is called today" (L, II, 398-400).

36 See, e.g., Freud, Interpretation of Dreams, pp. 493-494.

37 Jung, Memories, Dreams, Reflections, p. 237. 38 Fromm, The Forgotten Language, p. 47.

39 Cf. a brief report, August 15, 1838, one month after the Divinity School Address: "I woke this morning with saying or thinking in my dream that every truth appealed to a heroic character. This does not seem to hold of mathematical as of ethical science" (J, V, 13).

40 Stephen Whicher presented the opposite position, i.e., that the dominant mood of the mature Emerson is one of skepticism and/or despair, in his brilliant Freedom and Fate (Philadelphia, 1953). John Lydenberg relates Emerson to such writers as Poe, Melville, Hemingway, and Faulkner, in a challenging analysis of "Experience" (Critical Quarterly, IV [Winter, 1962], 352-358).

41 Edwin Diamond, The Science of Dreams (Garden City, 1862), pp. 210-221. Cf. Ellis Freeman, Principles of General Psychology (N.Y., 1939), p. 500.

42 For a penetrating analysis of this theory in Bacon and Milton, see Edward Le Comte, Endymion in England: The Literary History of a Greek Myth (N.Y., 1944), pp. 127-129.

43 Mircea Eliade, Myths, Dreams and Mysteries (N.Y., 1960), pp. 105-108. 44 Memoir, I, 221.

45 Of the dreamer touching a part of his body during sleep, Scott writes: "He is clearly, in this case, both the actor and patient, both the proprietor of the member touching, and of that which is touched...." (Lectures on Demonology and Witchcraft [London, 1884], p. 43).

46 Ralph Cudworth, The True Intellectual System of the Universe, 4 vols. (London, 1820), I, 247. Bacon had a strange prophetic dream of his father's death, but his view of this kind of dream in the essay "Of Prophecies" is skeptical (Essays, Works, ed. James Spedding et alia, 14 vols. [London, 1857-1874], IV, 463-465). 47 Fromm, The Forgotten Language, p. 139.

48 For a full study of Plutarch's influence, see Edmund G. Berry, Emerson's Plutarch (Cambridge, 1961).

49 William E. Bridges, "Transcendentalism and Psychotherapy: Another Look at Emerson," AL, XLI (May, 1969), 157-177.

R. W. EMERSON SAMUEL BRADFORD WILLIAM H. FURNESS

From a photograph by Gutekunst, Philadelphia, in 1875

CHARLES CHAUNCY EMERSON.

R. W. EMERSON, [TAKEN ABOUT 1843.]

EDWARD BLISS EMERSON.

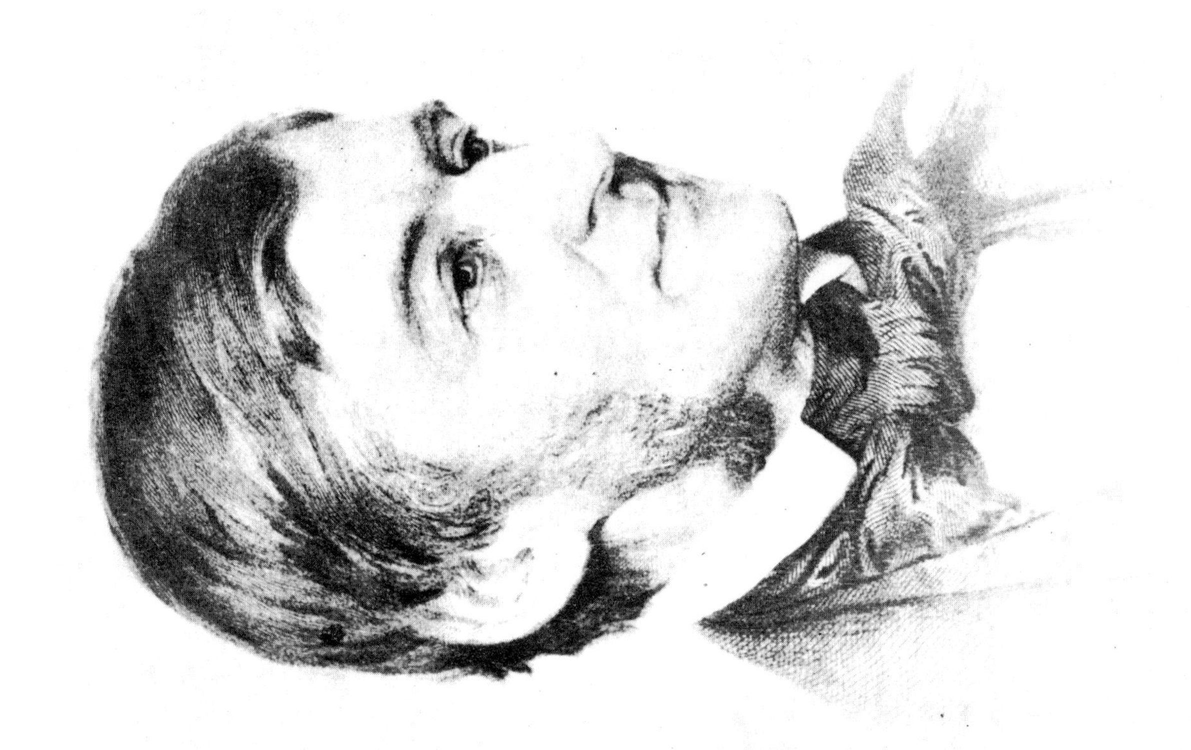

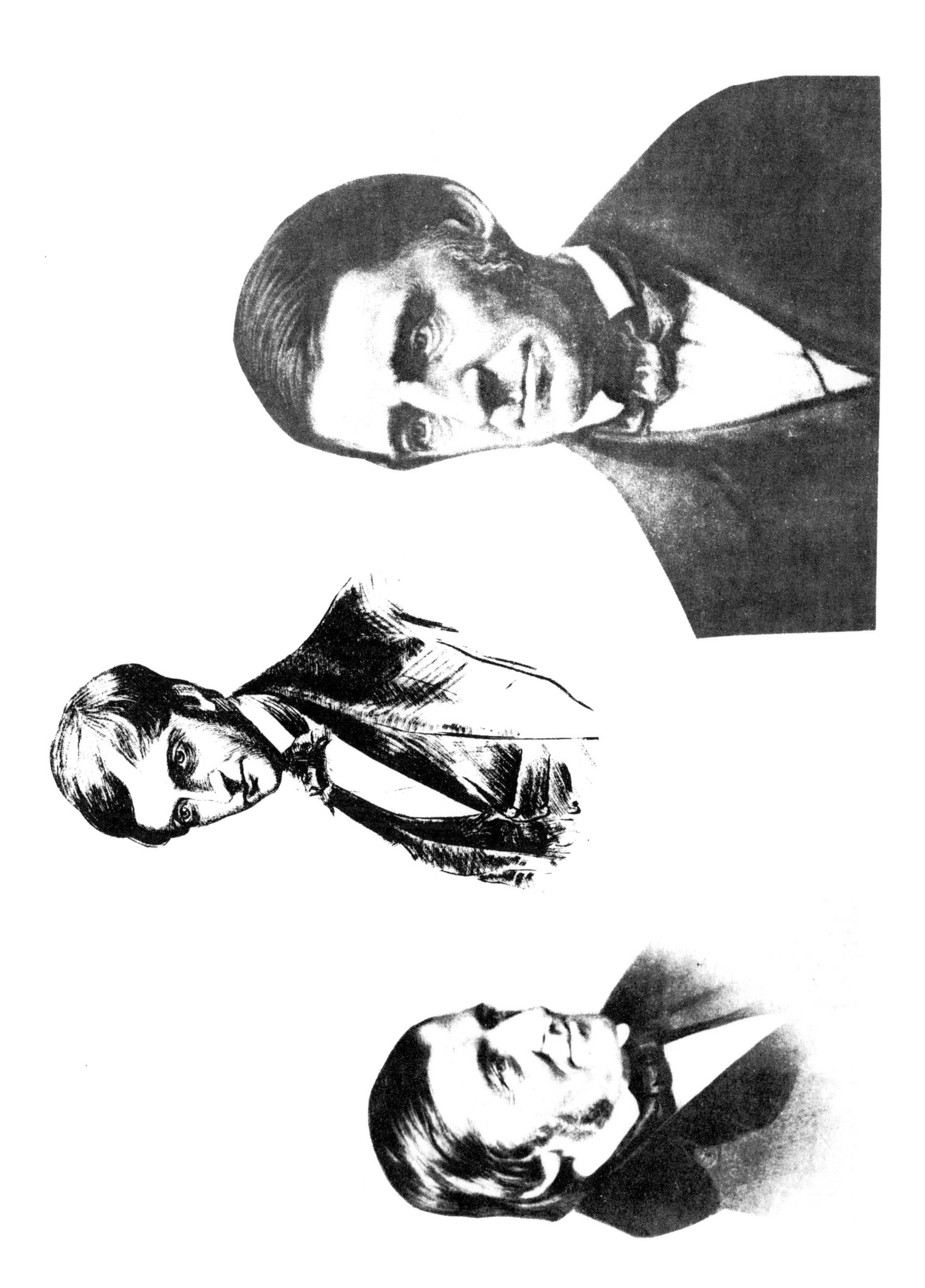

EMERSON

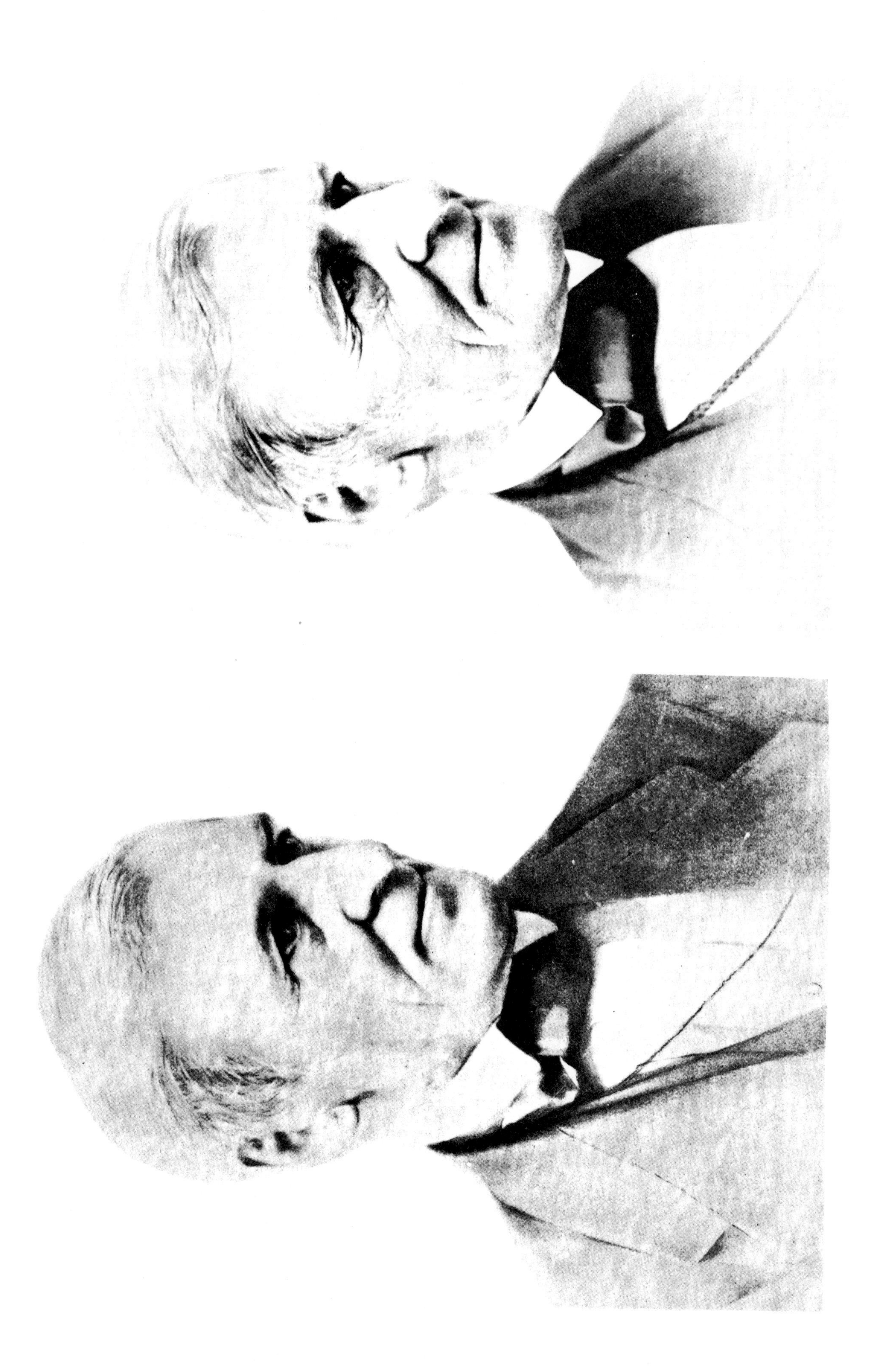